TRANSFORMATIONAL THINKING

For Transformational Leadership
and Christian Scholarship

Ralph L. Dennis

Copyright © 2015 by Ralph L. Dennis

Transformational Thinking
For Transformational Leadership and Christian Scholars
by Ralph L. Dennis

Printed in the United States of America.

ISBN 9781498438322

All rights reserved solely by the author. The author guarantees all contents are original and do not infringe upon the legal rights of any other person or work. No part of this book may be reproduced in any form without the permission of the author. The views expressed in this book are not necessarily those of the publisher.

Unless otherwise indicated, Scripture quotations taken from the King James Version (KJV) – public domain.

www.xulonpress.com

TABLE OF CONTENTS

Introduction- Transformational Thinking vii

Chapter 1 Transformational Thinking and Transformational
Leadership. 13
The Gateway
Transformational Thinkers
Transformational Leadership
Designing Transformational Leader Development
The Design

Chapter 2 Transformational Thinking 21

Chapter 3 Transformational Thinking—Nurturing the
Leader's Inner Life 34

Chapter 4 Three Perspectives of Transformation 38

Chapter 5 Transformational Thinkers are Chosen 44

Chapter 6 Identifying the Plan of God for Your Life. 52

Chapter 7 Moving into the Place Beyond 59

Chapter 8 Wrong Thinking 66

Chapter 9 Prophetic Imagination. 75

Chapter 10	Transformational Thinking and Christian Scholarship 79
Chapter 11	Holy Intelligence (HQ) and the Bible 87
Chapter 12	Transformation as the Center of New Testament Theology 99
Chapter 13	Transformational Leadership 105
Chapter 14	Transformational Thinking is Healthy Thinking 113
Chapter 15	Rules of Engagement: Connecting the Dots 118
Chapter 16	Choosing the Right Emerging Transformational Leaders 122

INTRODUCTION

The principles of this book are based on a few primary scriptures, though many more will be explored:

Proverbs 23:7 King James Version

For as he thinketh in his heart, so is he: eat and drink, saith he to thee; but his heart is not with thee.

Matthew 11:12 New International Version

From the days of John the Baptist until now, the kingdom of heaven has been subjected to violence, and violent people have been raiding it.

Revelation 11:15 New King James Version

Then the seventh angel sounded: And there were loud voices in heaven, saying, "The kingdoms, of this world have become the kingdoms of our Lord and of His Christ, and He shall reign forever and ever!"

1 Chronicles 12:32 New King James Version

Of the sons of Issachar who had understanding of the times, to know what Israel ought to do, their chiefs were two hundred; and all their brethren were at their command;

These texts may seem a little odd when you consider transformational thinking, but unless the body of Christ yields to the transforming power of the Holy Spirit, we will not be like the sons of Issachar nor will we be able to withstand the onslaught of the enemy and see the kingdoms of this world become the kingdoms of our Lord and of His Christ.

Our focus must be to transform our thinking. Transform means to change radically in inner character, conditions or nature. Transformational thinking is radical thinking. Radical thinking is not rational; it is God thinking. God's thoughts toward us are thoughts of peace and not evil. He says that He will give us an expected end. In the natural, we may see decay and failure, but when we transform our thinking, we see growth, success and abundance. When we transform our thinking, we see ourselves in an ascended posture where what is going on in the Spirit realm outweighs our circumstances, and our responses are spiritual and not carnal. God provides us with an example in that when we give Him our natural situations, He gives us spiritual solutions. For us to respond spiritually each time, we must engage in transformational thinking.

The word *transformational* is an adjective. The root is transform. I chose to use it as an adjective in this book because it describes the kind of thinking we must have. God does not want us to just have thoughts, but He wants us to have transformational thoughts. Our thinking has a lot to do with our behavior, experiences and relationships. The way we think can hinder the manifestation of the Lord's will for our lives. The concept of the book "Think and Grow Rich" (Napoleon Hill, 1938 ed.) was that your wealth has to do with how you think. He made this claim, "whatever your mind can conceive and believe it can achieve." Bad thinking will keep us from optimizing in our place with God and will cause us to repeat lessons.

The biblical concept of transformation has become universal and can be heard in almost any setting, spiritual and secular, among Christian and non-Christians. There are pastors who are lauded as transformation pastors and churches that have undergone transformation, but what does that mean? If a person gets transformed or a church goes through the transformational process, what happens in that process? It goes beyond sanctification to an orchestrated, systemic and revolutionary transformation of societies, churches, the marketplace and every kingdom of the world. It is more than a change in liturgy, worship styles, new technologies and smarter leaders; rather it is a re-forging of the foundations of Protestantism, western civilization and the governance of the entire world.

Transformational thinking goes far beyond changes that have taken us from oxen to tractors, from typewriters to tablet; from albums to MP3s; from pay phones in public places to cell phones in every pocket. Transformational thinking refers to an all-encompassing kingdom view which sees, prophesies, and foreordains and where the saints are orchestrating systemic change which forces every portion of society to adapt to changes ordained by God.

Daniel 7:18-22 supports this thought.

> *¹⁸ But the saints of the Most High shall receive the kingdom, and possess the kingdom forever, even forever and ever.'*
>
> *¹⁹ "Then I wished to know the truth about the fourth beast, which was different from all the others, exceedingly dreadful, with its teeth of iron and its nails of bronze, which devoured, broke in pieces, and trampled the residue with its feet; ²⁰ and the ten horns that were on its head, and the other horn which came up, before which three fell, namely, that horn which had eyes and a mouth which spoke pompous words, whose appearance was greater than his fellows.*
>
> *²¹ "I was watching; and the same horn was making war against the saints, and prevailing against them, ²² until the Ancient of Days came, and a judgment was made in favor of the saints of the Most High, and the time came for the saints to possess the kingdom.*

There are several points that need to be highlighted relative to this passage:

1. Transformational thinking shifts the focus of the church from the pulpit to the pew/saints
2. Transformational thinking shifts the power of the church from the church to the kingdom of God.

3. Transformational thinking shifts the dominion authority of the church from the nuclear church to the marketplace.
4. Transformational thinking produces kingdom manifestations as believers are challenged to revisit and reexamine perspective areas of transformation:
a. Psychological- a change in the understanding of self
b. Convictional- revisiting and when needed, revising our belief system
c. Behavioral – change in lifestyles and choices we make

Transformational thinking broadens believers' perceptions of God's will for the world, so that we are better suited to optimize our spheres of influence. In accordance to Matthew 9:17, believers who embrace transformational thinking will not spend lots of time trying to force new wine into old bottles, but will put the new wine in new bottles and ensure both the new and the old are preserved.

Chapter 1

Transformational Thinking and Transformational Leadership

Transformational thinking is the gateway to thorough and dramatic change in every aspect of your life. The philosophy, skills and personal attributes that underpin transformational thinking are used extensively in developing advanced capabilities in the contexts of leadership, personal performance, and professional coaching.

Transformational thinking is the release of old thinking and the adoption of radically new ways of thinking and behaving in order to achieve a quantum leap in results. Success depends, among other things, on the willingness to risk making decisions based not on past experience, but on the possibility of a different reality.

There are some critical and sophisticated new skills required to be able to look back from a future point, and to skillfully and successfully execute the transformation required to bring that imagined future into being.

Transformational thinking can be applied in all areas of life, work, and relationships. It is this universal application that allows us to engage people to make transformation work, and to develop enhanced resilience, optimism and resolve in the entire organization. Transformational thinking is an approach to life, work, and play, which is based on personal accountability, authenticity and vision. Its basic tenets are simple, seemingly universal, truths which enable individuals and teams to create generative change, build sustainable success, and perform at their optimum, in any circumstance. Transformational thinking connects who you are, with how you perform.

Whilst the approach is simple, execution tends not to be so easy. Most people have been conditioned to think, feel and act in ways which are inherently self-limiting and disempowering – encouraged to think that success is driven by what they DO, and measured by what they HAVE. As a result, they struggle constantly to DO more, so they may HAVE more. Transformational thinking proposes that success in any life area is driven by WHO YOU ARE, and is measured by how well you PERFORM in that area. Our invitation is for you to discover the best you can BE, and the incredible difference you can make when you optimize your PERFORMANCE throughout your life roles. Explained simply, transformational thinking connects who you are, with how you perform.

Transformational Leaders

When transformational thinking is applied in the sphere of leadership, we get transformational leadership. Transformational leaders derive authority and power from their authenticity based on character, not their position or role. Transformational leaders rally people to a cause or vision with their passion and conviction. Trustworthy, believable, passionate, inspiring, and confident people are attractive to followers. Transformational leadership is not learned in a training program or course, it is the outcome of a personal journey towards authentic leadership, allied to passion, belief, and the determination to achieve something worthwhile.

Designing Transformational Leader Development [1]

Let's look at how to design transformational leader development. Transformational leader development requires more than classroom instruction. Life transformation takes place through a combination of the Four Dynamics of Transformation:

- *Spiritual Dynamics* – include prayer, worship, reflection, meditation in the Word;
- *Relational Dynamics* – include encouragement, accountability, examples, mentors, coaches;
- *Experiential Dynamics* – include learning by doing, challenging assignments, and pressure;
- *Instructional Dynamics* – include the teaching of the Word of God in an engaging and interactive way.

Traditional training, however, almost exclusively uses the Instructional Dynamic. Consequently, when we design training, it largely consists of putting together a lot of content. We give considerable attention to making sure the content is accurate and balanced and that it is delivered in the right order and so forth. Traditionally, designing training essentially means to *prepare content*.

---

[1] http://www.leadershipletters.com/category/transformational-leader-development-design/

If we shift to a holistic 4D process, of course we will still need well-designed content, but we will also need *good design of the other three dynamics*. We can see this in Jesus' ministry: He gave a great deal of design focus to the spiritual, relational and experiential dynamics.

To do this requires a significant shift in thinking from traditional curricular approaches. We must think more broadly about training design. We cannot limit our design to the content; we must also deliberately incorporate design for the other three dynamics. Jesus designed relationships, experiences, responsibilities, challenges, pressures, all sorts of things – and all of it worked together well to bring life transformation to His disciples.

When a chef prepares a dish, he knows what he intends the final product to look, smell and taste like. He starts with the goal and then he determines the ingredients, the order in which they are added, how they should be mixed together and how it should be cooked – all the details of the design. This is how we can design training. We can have a written curriculum or a written design that gives us direction about how to move forward in providing all four dynamics of transformation. The written design will show us the various ingredients and how they are mixed together.

Jesus didn't have a written curriculum; He didn't need it. He lived in perfect, unbroken fellowship with His Father. From His Father, He always knew the right thing to do moment by moment. However, we need this kind of design.

Prepared Design and Responsive Design

Jesus did essentially two kinds of leader development. First, He would design relationships, responsibilities and so forth in advance, and then He would lead His disciples through those experiences and teachings. This is "prepared design."

We also see a second kind of design when things spontaneously happened around him and then He interacted with those opportunities in a way that was transformational for His disciples. Thus, some designs were *prepared* in advance while other times He *responded* to what happened. However, in both cases there was purpose and intentionality. Jesus was always thinking about what was happening and how He could use it as an opportunity for life transformation.

If we have a strong understanding of the principles of transformational leader development, we can do both. We can prepare designs in advance and we can also respond well to whatever happens spontaneously in the complex process of life.

Transformational Leader Development Design

Probably everybody who is reading these words has the ability to sit in a car and be driven somewhere by someone else. Everybody can benefit from the car. Whether or not we understand how the car works or even how to drive it, we can benefit from it. But how many people can drive the car? Quite a few, but not everyone. Then, how many people can change the oil in the car and do basic maintenance work? This is a significantly smaller group. How many people can fix the engine when it breaks down? Even fewer.

Now, think about when the car was built. How many people have the knowledge and skills to work on the production line and produce the car? Very few. Then, how many people have the ability to precisely engineer the various parts of the car? Not many. Finally, how many people can invent something like a car in the first place? Hardly anyone.

In another analogy, very few people can write a truly great book, but multitudes can read it and benefit from it. Leader development is like this. While everyone can do simple design, God has given the church a few people who can create complex design. We need to identify those who can design strong four-dynamic leader development processes that are appropriate for the church in a certain context – those who understand the church and the people, those who know the culture, the language, and the particular needs. There are only a few people with this specific calling to create a design that others can use.

Most people can implement complex design – as long as it is articulated clearly. In this way, we can build a unified leader development culture and practice across the life of the church. Such a model provides a unifying language and framework for this, so that everyone understands what we are doing, why we are doing it, and how we are doing it. Everyone can fully cooperate and the body will be enhanced.

In the church, God has called some to do this and some to do that (1 Cor. 12). Even when Christ ascended on high and gave gifts to men, they varied; He gave some apostles, some prophets, some evangelists, and some pastors and teachers (Ephesians 4:11). When we all function within our callings, the body is built up.

<u>One Size Does Not Fit All</u>

The church in every culture and context needs designers of leader development. It is not realistic that curriculum developed in one place will work everywhere for everyone. There are simply too many variables, such as culture, education level, background, socio-economic factors, current specific needs, etc. Moreover, things constantly change, so a design that worked well in the past may not work today.

Instead of trying to create a single curriculum for everyone to use, we should nurture leaders' capacity to design their own leader development. Some will emerge as specialist designers for complex design, while others will be able to do simple design.

Reconnecting Leader Development with Life

This is not to imply that every designer must create everything from nothing. In every situation, we already have great resources from which we can draw. We already have some great content that needs to be "reframed" or reconfigured in a holistic way so it is not just content and lectures. Everyone already has spiritual, relational and experiential opportunities – we just need to interact with them in an intentional, well-designed way.

Every church and ministry already have vast ministry opportunities, working with children, young people, families and older people. Every church is already doing a lot in pastoral work, evangelism, even church planting and missions work. There are challenges and opportunities on every hand! All of these ministries are not just tasks that need to be done – they are opportunities in which we can build people.

Every church and ministry already have relational opportunities. There are men and women of God with deep experience in God who we can be intentionally connecting with others as role models and in mentoring roles. There are coaches who can be mobilized in leadership development work. There are endless spiritual opportunities with which to interface.

This is a shift of thinking. Traditionally, we have taken the training work, pulled it out of its context of life and made it stand by itself.

This has not worked. We must reconnect leader development with life. Everyone can do it. Everyone must do it!

Summary of Transformational Leadership

Transformational leaders build communities that lean toward the future. Such communities look beyond the tasks of today to the opportunities of tomorrow. Ultimately, this means that transformational leaders focus considerable attention on issues of legacy, which is always about the work of intentionally raising up future community leaders.

For the vision demands that the community not only endure, but flourish in years, decades, and centuries to come. It is incumbent on each generation of transformational servants to identify and develop the next generation of transformational servants.

Chapter 2

Transformational Thinking

The first element of transformational thinking is looking at God. The continuous experience of inward union with Christ is the source and center of all other healthy thinking behaviors.

I want to know Christ… (Phil. 3:10) This was Paul's cry, his passionate pursuit. To know the Lord Jesus is the greatest prize, far surpassing everything else in this life (Phil. 3:4-9).

Jesus defined "eternal life" the same way: eternal life is to know God. *Now this is eternal life: that they may know you, the only true God, and Jesus Christ, whom you have sent. (John 17:3)* But, what exactly does it mean to "know" Jesus Christ? What does it mean to "know" God?

<u>Knowing God</u>

In the world, there are many ideas about what it means to "know God." Here are a few:

- To know God is to serve others.
- To know God is to obey moral rules.
- To know God is to perform religious rituals.

- To know God is to have an accurate understanding about Him.
- To know God is to sense the beauty and grandeur of His creation.
- To know God is to feel the passion and depth of the arts.
- To know God is to experience wonderful emotions of peace and joy.
- To know God is to achieve an inward state of freedom from selfish desires.
- To know God is to receive forgiveness of sins and then passively wait for eternity in heaven after death.

According to each of these various approaches, if you do this then you "know God." To do it *means* to know God.

According to the New Testament, however, none of these definitions is satisfactory. Biblically, knowing Christ is the gift from God of an inward experience of fellowship with Him, by His Spirit and through His Word, which results in the transformation of every aspect of life.

First, it is *His gift*. We can know Jesus because, by His death on the cross, He paid the penalty for our sins, reconciling us to God.

... since we have been justified through faith, we have peace with God through our Lord Jesus Christ, through whom we have gained access by faith into this grace in which we now stand... God has poured out his love into our hearts by the Holy Spirit, whom he has given us. (Rom. 5:1-5) It is the gift of God – and it is always His gift – that we can know Him. We do not earn fellowship with God. He gives Himself to us. Throughout our lives we *grow* in our union with Christ, ; we never earn *it* – whether by external obedience or inward spiritual exercise.

Therefore, brothers, since we have confidence to enter the Most Holy Place by the blood of Jesus, by a new and living way opened for us through the curtain, that is, his body, and since we have a great priest over the house of God, let us draw near to God with a sincere heart in full assurance of faith, having our hearts sprinkled to cleanse us from a guilty conscience and having our bodies washed with pure water. (Heb. 10:19-22)

Second, while knowing God is an experience, it is not an emotional, intellectual or physical one (although it will impact these aspects of life). *In our hearts*, we look at God, we receive His love, we love Him, and we know Him.

And we all, with unveiled face [in our hearts, v. 15], *beholding the glory of the Lord, are being transformed into the same image from one degree of glory to another. For this comes from the Lord who is the Spirit. (2 Cor. 3:18, ESV)*

Third, it is *by the Holy Spirit*. The Holy Spirit reveals to us the Son of God who reveals the Father. *All that belongs to the Father is mine. That is why I said the Spirit will take from what is mine and make it known to you. (John 16:15)* Consequently, through the indwelling Spirit we have the fullness of the Godhead abiding in us!

Fourth, we find inward union with God *through His Word*. The Word of God reveals Him in truth and power. *We proclaim to you what we have seen and heard, so that you also may have fellowship with us. And our fellowship is with the Father and with his Son, Jesus Christ. (1 John 1:3)*

Finally, knowing God *results in transformation* of all we are and do (Rom. 6:1-4). This will mean peace with God (Rom. 5:1), obedience (John 14:15; 1 John 3:24), holiness (Rom. 8:3-4; 1 John 2:3-6), vision and fruitfulness (John 15:5), passion for the lost (2 Cor. 5:20), endurance with hope in times of suffering (2 Cor. 4:16-18), zealous ministry work (1 Cor. 15:10), and love and servanthood toward others (Gal. 5:13-14).

Therefore, if anyone is in Christ, he is a new creation; the old has gone, the new has come! (2 Cor. 5:17) Our fellowship is with the Father and with His Son, Jesus Christ.

That which was from the beginning, which we have heard, which we have seen with our eyes, which we have looked at and our hands have touched – this we proclaim concerning the Word of life. The life appeared; we have seen it and testify to it, and we proclaim to you the eternal life, which was with the Father and has appeared to us. We proclaim to you what we have seen and heard, so that you also may have fellowship with us. And our fellowship is with the Father and with his Son, Jesus Christ. (1 John 1:1-3)

In the beginning of the first chapter of his first epistle, John sets forth his principal motivation in preaching the Gospel. It was not his motivation only, but it has been that of all true servants of God, then and since.

What could this motivation be to cause these men to endure hardships, persecutions, beatings, stonings, imprisonments, journeys, perils, shipwrecks, misunderstandings, betrayals, weariness, painfulness, watchings, hunger and thirst, fastings, cold and nakedness? What could this passion be that those consumed by it would forsake all worldly fortune and pleasure and seek to take the Gospel to others? Surely, it must be their concern for man's deliverance from an eternal hell! Surely, no other purpose could justify such sufferings as the true servants of God have experienced historically! Surprisingly, this was not their primary motivation.

Stated here in First John is the reason why these men proclaimed the Gospel to us; namely, that we may have fellowship "with them", meaning that we may have the *same* fellowship that they had, and that "is with the Father, and with His Son Jesus Christ." Please notice that John did not say that his fellowship "was" with God, but that his fellowship "is" with God. Through the indwelling Holy Spirit, John experienced a vital union and communion with Christ long after Jesus had physically left the earth, and his objective was that we know that *same* fellowship.

Here was their passion, their all-consuming obsession, and the deepest desire of God's true servants in this our day: *to bring men to the personal knowledge of Jesus Christ and the Father.*

Furthermore, please notice what the fellowship is that John wants us to experience. Is it a purely theoretical knowledge of God that we should have? Is it simply an academic appreciation of the Biblical doctrines about the Son of God that we need to strive after? Is it merely an accurate understanding of the legal, judicial implications of the teachings of the New Testament that we must endeavor to achieve? God forbid!

John says that we should pursue the same *fellowship* with God that he experienced. What quality of fellowship was that? Listen closely as the apostle himself tells us about his own relationship with God, which level of relationship he desires that we all experience: "That which was from the beginning (i.e. the eternal God), which we have *heard,* which we have *seen with our eyes,* which we have *looked at* and our *hands have touched.*" Here was the reality of John's experience with God: he heard Him, he looked upon Him and he even *touched* Him! This was John's fellowship with his Lord. It was real. It was tangible. It was a deep experience of fellowship with his Master.

John touched the eternal God, his hands handled Him! He rested his head upon God's bosom. Obviously John had no physical contact with eternal, infinite, transcendent Spirit, yet he *did* touch God. *Great is the glory and the mystery of godliness: God was manifested in the flesh, and dwelt among men.* The eternal God whom no man can look upon and live; the great infinite Spirit who dwells in light unapproachable; the unchanging, omnipotent, omniscient, omnipresent Creator of the universe was born of a woman and tabernacled among us. This is the glory and the wonder of the Incarnation. The invisible God now has an image. The Father whom no man has ever seen is now revealed (Col. 1:15; Heb. 1:3; John 14:7-9; 15:24).

Emmanuel – the Hebrew word for "God is (personally present) with us – walks among men. Man once again can have personal fellowship with his God. This is why John preached the Gospel: that we might be restored to fellowship with God; and not just to a legal, theoretical relationship with God, but to a fellowship as solid and as "tangible" as the close friendship that John himself enjoyed with the Savior.

In fact, we have been called to an *even deeper inward fellowship* with God than what Jesus' disciples enjoyed while He was on the earth:

...it is for your good that I am going away. Unless I go away, the Comforter will not come to you; but if I go, I will send him to you. (John 16:7)

I will not leave you as orphans; I will come to you. (John 14:18 NET)

We may be tempted to be jealous of the companionship the disciples had with our Lord, but really we are not offered anything less than what they had. The communion we can experience with Jesus through His indwelling Spirit, is more abiding and deeper than a mere physical closeness. "*Christ in you*" is our new life (Col. 1:27).

This is what we are called to. Our summons from the Great Eternal King is to know Him, to experience Him, to enjoy Him and to possess Him.

God is faithful, who has called you into fellowship with his Son, Jesus Christ our Lord. (1 Cor. 1:9)

This is what the Christian life is: restoration to fellowship with God. The experience of this should be our highest aspiration and this is the source of true Christian leadership.

Beholding God

Our last section looked at the first, and most important, element of transformational thinking: To Know God. Biblically, knowing the Lord Jesus is the gift from God of an inward experience of fellowship with Him, by His Spirit and through His Word, which results in the transformation of every aspect of life. *Now this is eternal life: that they may know you, the only true God, and Jesus Christ, whom you have sent. (John 17:3)*

Knowing God is not merely an intellectual agreement about a "legal position" in Christ, but it is to be a conscious, inward *experience* of fellowship with Him: *...He who loves me will be loved by my Father, and I too will love him and show myself to him. (John 14:21)*

That which was from the beginning, which we have heard, which we have seen with our eyes, which we have looked at and our hands have touched... We proclaim to you what we have seen and heard, so that you also may have fellowship with us. And our fellowship is with the Father and with his Son, Jesus Christ. (1 John 1:1-3)

Sadly, a traditional idea in some churches is that the presence of the Holy Spirit in our hearts is something that we only ever take "by faith." We simply believe that we have His indwelling presence, whether or not we are ever actually *conscious* of it. As a result, Christianity becomes somewhat of an intellectual and theoretical exercise. We mentally agree with what God has said and it stops there; our lives then consist of gritting our teeth and trying to do, in our own strength, what we know God wants us to do. Of course, theory will only satisfy us for so long. In the end, it becomes frustrating; our theory tells us about all the wonderful things that we should be experiencing, but we are not experiencing. Consequently, the more theory we have, the more frustrated we become.

To have a transformed and victorious life, we need His presence. This inward experience of God is mentioned frequently in the New Testament: *And we all, with unveiled face* [in our hearts, v. 15], *beholding the glory of the Lord, are being transformed into the same image from one degree of glory to another. For this comes from the Lord who is the Spirit. (2 Cor. 3:18, ESV)*

In our hearts, we look at God, we receive His love, we love Him, we know Him; and this union with Christ is the foundation and wellspring of everything in our lives and ministries. *Because you are sons, God sent the Spirit of his Son into our hearts, the Spirit who calls out, "Abba, Father." (Gal. 4:6)*

The Holy Spirit is not simply an unfelt and theoretical presence that we accept by faith. In our hearts, He cries out "Abba, Father." The Spirit loves the Father and the Son, just as He has done for all eternity. The eternal fellowship of the Godhead is happening in our hearts! *Those who obey his commands live in him, and he in them. And this is how we know that he lives in us: We know it by the Spirit he gave us. (1 John 3:24)*

John says we know God lives in us by the presence of His Spirit in our hearts. This does not refer to mere mental agreement, but to an inward spiritual perception, a conscious awareness of His presence. *We know that we live in him and he in us, because he has given us of his Spirit. (1 John 4:13)*

Anyone who believes in the Son of God has this testimony in his heart... (1 John 5:10)

But the Counselor, the Holy Spirit, whom the Father will send in my name, will teach you all things and will remind you of everything I have said to you. (John 14:26)

But when he, the Spirit of truth, comes, he will guide you into all truth. He will not speak on his own; he will speak only what he hears, and he will tell you what is yet to come. He will bring glory to me by taking from what is mine and making it known to you. All that belongs to the Father is mine. That is why I said the Spirit will take from what is mine and make it known to you. (John 16:13-15)

... God has poured out his love into our hearts by the Holy Spirit, whom he has given us. (Rom. 5:5)

...those who are led by the Spirit of God are sons of God. (Rom. 8:14)

The Spirit himself testifies with our spirit that we are God's children. (Rom. 8:16)

These, and other New Testament passages, are clear and dramatic. The Holy Spirit will 'testify," "remind," "guide," "speak," "tell," 'Make it known," and "lead." Moreover, this is not only an occasional thing; we can know His presence *continuously,* in the midst of suffering as well as blessing: *...If anyone loves me, he will obey my teaching. My Father will love him, and we will come to him and make our home with him. (John 14:23)*

The Holy Spirit is with us. He is in us, crying out "Abba Father," revealing the love of the Father, and the glory of the Son.

This is the living nucleus of transformational thinking: the inward experience of fellowship with God, by His Spirit. Every other aspect of our thinking, and our lives, must revolve around this – around Him.

Loving God

This section introduces a new model of transformational thinking from the baseline of loving God. *Love the Lord your God with all your heart and with all your soul and with all your mind and with all your strength. (Mark 12:30)*

To "*love God with all your mind*" means to fully *explore* and *use* the thinking capacities He has given you, in a manner always proceeding from, and subject to, His indwelling presence. This will result in true, self-giving love toward others: *...Love your neighbor as yourself... (Mark 12:31)*

The Fall and Rise of the Mind of Man

God created man to be a brilliant thinker. After his creation in God's image, man had the ability to know His Creator – to look at Him, to fellowship with Him, to love Him – and to serve Him with highly complex thinking capacities.

When he sinned, man died spiritually (Gen. 2:17; Eph. 2:1, 5), becoming alienated from God's life and truth (Col. 1:21). The image of God in man was deeply marred, and his thinking became "futile:" empty and worthless.

...their thinking became futile and their foolish hearts were darkened. Although they claimed to be wise, they became fools. (Rom. 1:21-22; cf. Ps. 94:11)

Consequently, even though fallen man is still capable of complex and sophisticated thinking, by virtue of his creation in God's image, it is but a faint and distorted shadow of his original thinking capacities. Thus, man can split the atom, but builds atomic bombs; he can create the internet, but disperses pornography and violence on it, he can produce intricate pieces of art, but they are idolatrous and blasphemous; he can shape brilliant analysis, but uses it to deceive others. *...out of the heart come evil thoughts, murder, adultery, sexual immorality, theft, false testimony, slander. (Matt. 15:19)*

Thank God, He did not abandon us to our own corrupt and futile ways! Through Jesus' death and resurrection, we can be reconciled to God, and restored to union with Him. From His indwelling life, through the power of His truth, our minds are then progressively "renewed" (Rom. 12:2) and our thinking capacities restored to the true image of God (Col. 3:10).

As we daily choose to walk in "new life" (Rom. 6:4), counting ourselves "dead to sin but alive to God" (Rom. 6:11), we can have the "mind of Christ" (1 Cor. 2:16)! Thus, our thinking is transformed and God can use us as His agents of transformation for others.

How Leaders Think

Essentially, leaders do two things: they *think* and *act*. To be successful, they must do both well.

Many writings about leadership (ours included) have appropriately focused on the leader's many and varied actions, such as communication, leading change, team-building, conflict management, collaboration, delegation, building leaders, and so forth. This model of transformational thinking focuses on the inward life of the leader – how he thinks – the fountainhead of his actions. While it is vital to give attention to the *content* of thinking (*what* we think), we must also attend to the *processes* of thinking (*how* we think).

Transformational Thinking

This model identifies *ten critical thinking capacities of a healthy Christian leader*. These behaviors are distinct from each other, but there is much overlap and interaction between them. Usually, integrated clusters of them will work together in various situations.

Let me now mention ten habits of transformational thinking:[2]

1. *Looking at God*. The continuous experience of inward union with Christ is the source and center of all other healthy thinking behaviors.
2. *Passion for the Highest.* The leader must always strive to grow, to solve, to build, and to overcome – always pressing on to fulfill God's purposes.
3. *Love of Learning*. Transformational thinking explores, questions, and continuously learns.
4. *Learning from Mistakes*. The leader must be resilient, flexible and adaptable--able to learn from their own mistakes.
5. *Thinking about Thinking*. Reflection and evaluation help the leader maintain accurate self-awareness and avoid self-deception and unnecessary limitations.
6. *Embracing Ambiguity*. Leadership is rarely straightforward and clear, so the leader must be willing and able not only to tolerate ambiguity, but actually to embrace paradox and uncertainty as the indispensable authors of new insights, solutions and opportunities.
7. *Thinking Interdependently*. Together we are complete. The leaders must value and be sensitive and accountable to those

---

[2] http://www.leadershipletters.com/2009/11/13/loving-god-with-our-minds/

around him. To think well, he needs to think in cooperation with others.

8. *Engaging Deeply.* Healthy leaders fully participate in the world around them. To understand joy, sorrow, beauty, pain, victory and divine life, the leader must experience them.
9. *Integrating Science and Art.* Healthy thinkers develop and use both discipline and creativity – both logic and innovation – to solve problems and explore opportunities.
10. *Thinking Holistically.* A key leadership capacity is to see the big picture --integrating spiritual and practical, identifying and analyzing both internal and external patterns, and recognizing how each part relates to the whole.

This is *transformational thinking!* Such internal habits can transform our lives and the lives of those around us.

Our hope is that this model will present these thinking behaviors in a clear, unified, Christ-centered framework that enables us to more systematically and comprehensively nurture and use these habits as we live (thinking and acting well) out of Jesus' indwelling life for His glory.

CHAPTER 3

TRANSFORMATIONAL THINKING – NURTURING THE LEADER'S INNER LIFE

In Romans 8, Paul contrasts the old inner life with the new inner life in Christ:

For those who live according to the flesh set their minds on the things of the flesh, but those who live according to the Spirit set their minds on the things of the Spirit. For to set the mind on the flesh is death, but to set the mind on the Spirit is life and peace. (Rom. 8:5-6, ESV)

Here is a clear description of the practical, internal "mechanics" of union with Christ. The maturing believer "sets his mind" on the Spirit and on "the things of the Spirit." This means to inwardly turn away from the things of the old life (self, sin, the world, the devil) and to give our full inward attention to Him. This does not refer to our minds in a purely intellectual sense, but it means our *entire inward lives* – our minds, our hearts, our thoughts, our motivations, our affections, our love, our desires, our focus – "all that is within me..." (Ps. 103:1). It refers to the turning of our inward lives to Him. This is the internal mechanism of union with Christ, this is the internal activity of knowing God.

Since, then, you have been raised with Christ, set your hearts on things above, where Christ is seated at the right hand of God. Set your minds on things above, not on earthly things. (Col. 3:1-2) This is what it means to "draw near to God" (Heb. 10:22), to "seek [God] with all your heart" (Jer. 29:13), to "set the Lord always before me" (Ps. 16:8). We consciously and inwardly turn to Him, looking at Him, expecting Him to "look back." As we touch Him, He touches us!

Draw near to God, and He will draw near to you... (Jam. 4:8)

As we have seen in a previous chapter, the inward experience of fellowship with God is the living nucleus of transformational thinking and the source of everything good in the leader's life and ministry. Consequently, the leader must place the highest priority on nurturing this inner life. Union with Christ is the fountainhead of all true Christian leadership and ministry fruitfulness.

There are so many practical ways in which we can inwardly experience God and be nurtured by that experience. Here are a few:

- Praising God (Ps. 103; 150)
- Worshipping God (Ps. 29:2)
- Thanking God (Ps. 50:23)
- Loving God (Ps. 18:1)
- Receiving God's love (Ps. 33:22)
- Drawing near to God (Jam. 4:8)
- Appreciating God (Ps. 8:3-6)
- Resting in God (Ps. 62)
- Asking God (Ps. 43)
- Fearing God (Deut. 10:12)

Transformational Thinking

- Hoping in God (Ps. 33:20-22)
- Trusting in God (Ps. 33:21)
- Desiring God (Ps. 42)
- Yearning for God (Ps. 63:1)
- Hungering for God (Matt. 5:6)
- Pouring out your heart to God (1 Sam. 1:15)
- Sharing your complaints to God (Ps. 142)
- Telling God your struggles (Ps. 102)
- Repenting, turning to God, confessing your sins to Him (Ps. 51)
- Crying out to God (Ps. 4:1)
- Weeping before God (Ps. 30:5, 11)
- Submitting to God (Jam. 4:7)
- Proclaiming God's promises to Him (Ex. 32:13)
- Reading His Word (Ps. 1)
- Hoping in His Word (Ps. 119:114)
- Meditating on His Word (Ps. 119:148)
- Seeking God in His Word (Prov. 4:20; 5:1)
- Tearing your heart before God (Joel 2:13)
- Praying in the Spirit, praying with the understanding (1 Cor. 14:15)
- Singing in the Spirit, singing with the understanding (1 Cor. 14:15)
- Reflecting before God (2 Tim. 2:7)
- Remembering God's works (Ps. 77:11)
- Beholding His beauty (Ps. 27:4)
- Crying "Abba Father" (Rom. 8:15)

These actions are quite diverse, but they all share one thing in common: they are ways in which we inwardly *look at God*. In all these various ways, the leader inwardly turns – consciously and intentionally – to Him.

And we all, with unveiled face, beholding the glory of the Lord, are being transformed into the same image from one degree of glory to another… (2 Cor. 3:18, ESV)

So, turn to Him, look at Him, and inwardly reach to Him and as you do so, listen to Him, expect Him to speak, expect Him to reveal Himself to you, expect Him to touch you with His love. *…He who loves me will be loved by my Father, and I too will love him and show myself to him (John 14:21).*

The actions listed above can be done continuously, as well as during special focused times in the day. If you will do them – any of them, and even just a little – it will change your life, it will transform your leadership; and God will use you to profoundly impact the lives of many others!

Chapter 4

Three Perspectives of Transformation

Learned behavior can be a foe of transformational thinking. We are so habit driven that when it takes us out of the context of what has been then we feel like we are delving into heresy, but the reality is that we have never given ourselves limitlessly to God. Can you say, "I am unlimited in my faith?" There is some part of our natural being that likes to be in control. When we are asked to give ourselves limitlessly, it creates a dilemma for us because we like being in control. Transformational thinking, however, forces you to lose control and trust the Holy Spirit. If we are in control, then the Holy Spirit is not. Transformational thinking produces transformational manifestations. You cannot be a transformational thinker and get ordinary results. Transformational thinking produces transformational results. There are three perspectives of transformation: psychological, conviction and behavior.

The Psychological Perspective

A psychological perspective changes your understanding of self. Eastern religion promotes self as deity. Transformational thinking brings self into a fullness of who Christ has made you to be not as deity, but as the one created by God. I was created in the beginning, inasmuch as, all humans find their origin of creation and fall in Adam in the Garden of Eden. Likewise, we were recreated at Calvary, where the last Adam redeemed us from the fall of the first Adam. Thus, my ultimate paradigm is the Garden of Eden. The reflection of the garden is the cross of Calvary and what Jesus did for me. Transformational thinking deals with that part of us and helps us understand that we are new creatures. I have a new perspective because I understand that I have been redeemed. Transformational thinking causes me to be proud of self. Romans 12:2-4 admonishes us not to think *more highly* of ourselves than we ought, but we ought to think *highly*. Every believer should have a positive self- image. Failures may cloud our past experiences, but we ought to celebrate who are.

We cannot change our pasts so we should cease the effort. Investing time in trying to change the past is counterproductive. It is a waste of time and hinders our forward movement. If we understand the transformational power of God, we will not allow the past to dictate the future. Once we understand who we are we must develop a conviction.

The Six Christian Psychological Stages of Transformation[3]

Stage One: *Avoidance*: from the Christian perspective, it is Gethsemane. *"Father, if possible can this cup, please pass from Me."* Christ himself asked to avoid his reality even if for a moment.

Stage Two: *Surrender*: from the Christian perspective, it is Christ accepting His cross, His crucifixion and freely surrendering to the work at hand. *"Not my will but yours."* He accepted the process and began dismantling the old way.

Stage Three: *The Work*: from the Christian perspective, it is His death; His crucifixion. There is a death process in psychological transformation. Patients often dream of death, dying, destruction in this stage.

Stage Four: *Incubation*: from the Christian perspective, it is the time in the tomb. Christ descended into hell for three days. It is a time of confusion, chaos, and fear of the unknown. Everything is suspended.

Stage Five: *The Rebirth*: Christ is resurrected from the dead, and a fresh understanding begins for His followers. The new way has begun.

Stage Six: *Assimilation* of the new self: This is the Christian Ascension, when Christ takes on His transfigured body, and nothing in the world is ever the same.

The Convictional Perspective

Conviction has the ability to revise our beliefs. Our upbringing has left us quite limited in our understanding of being led by the Spirit. We have not been taught how to allow the Holy Spirit total access to our

---

[3] http://andrewdobo.com/2013/02/
six-stages-of-psychological-transformation-and-the-christian-parallel/

daily lives. If we had, we would not engage in certain behaviors or give certain responses. Our lack of conviction has limited our earthly effectiveness. God did not save us for heaven. The earth is our ultimate destiny. We were created to rule the earth.

Transformational thinking provokes us to reexamine our convictions and helps us to understand that we are to be kings and priests in the earth. We must reexamine our theology so we can apprehend where the Lord is trying to take us. When we get to heaven will everyone look like us and believe what we believe? We have a tendency to evaluate others based on what we believe. What we were taught has become our belief system. Transformational thinking can enlarge us so that we can possess the kingdom. We cannot possess the kingdom with a narrow belief system. The epitome of our belief system is that Christ is God; God made flesh. The deity of God is the epitome of our belief system, Christ is the redeemer. How we encounter that truth cannot be dictated by anyone else. Today, Christ would be ostracized for sitting in the pub among people who were smoking and drinking. Our theology would simply lead us to declare that light should have no fellowship with darkness without considering the reason why He was there. If you use that text, you assumed that He went in to fellowship as if He could not have been led there for purpose. The same applies to us. God calls us to fulfill purpose and He will determine what our purpose is. If it is a God purpose, we can stand undaunted by the criticism. Transformational thinking says we cannot fulfill our assignment based on another's belief.

I have a spiritual daughter who performs in secular plays and misses church, but I unequivocally released her to do it because entertainment is one of the kingdoms of this world. We must infiltrate it and we cannot change it by pointing to it and speaking in tongues. We have to go into all the world and make disciples wherever we are. You just have to understand why you are there. One of our elders was a radio host of a jazz program. During his sign off he would say, "Even if you don't love God; God loves you." This statement may have been all someone heard all week. Transformational thinking says no matter where I am, I am salt and light. Through the power of the Holy Spirit, I am in control of the environment while I am there.

Alignment and strength of conviction of the person to persist, stay the chosen path and the courage to deepen one's self awareness and readiness to change, are key to convictional transformation.

The Behavioral Perspective

Behavior change can refer to any transformation or modification of human behavior. Achieving sustained improvement in performance and lifestyle requires that organizations and individuals alike move beyond structures, processes, and systems to address individual and collective behavior—including culture, mind-sets and capabilities, and team and group dynamics. As a key aspect of creating transformational change, ministry and service to others must design and implement interventions to build skills, shift mind-sets, develop leaders, and manage talent to ensure a successful and sustainable change in behaviors.

There is a movie know as, "The Iron Lady." It was an excellent biographical portrayal of Great Britain's former Prime Minister, Margaret Thatcher. Her determination, decisiveness, and discipline gave her the edge she needed to ultimately become the first woman Prime Minister of Great Britain. The movie is definitely worth seeing and there were a number of quotes worth remembering. One of my favorite quotes from the movie was:

Watch your thoughts, they become words;
Watch your words, they become your actions;
Watch your actions, they become habits;
Watch your habits, they become character;
Watch your character, for it becomes your destiny.

Our thinking needs to change. Old thought patterns need to be replaced with new thoughts. Subtle lies that we once believed have to be exposed and replaced with truth. Our behavior is always driven by our beliefs. If I believe that I can drive 15 mph above the speed limit and get away with it, I will probably do that. The policeman is there to correct my belief system. After I have paid a couple of tickets and am threatened with losing my driver's license, I no longer believe I can speed without consequences. My behavior changes and I slow down. That's a weak illustration because I may still speed when I think the police are not around. But the point is this: My behavior is driven by my beliefs.

Behavioral Transformation is a relatively old concept which has been developed to help in organizational changes. In order to support change in organizations which are always linked to change in individual behavior, we use techniques to identify and support changes in programs and projects.

Chapter 5

Transformational Thinkers are Chosen for Key Assignments

Matthew 17:1-9 King James Version (KJV)

And after six days Jesus taketh Peter, James, and John his brother, and bringeth them up into an high mountain apart,[2] And was transfigured before them: and his face did shine as the sun, and his raiment was white as the light.[3] And, behold, there appeared unto them Moses and Elias talking with him.[4] Then answered Peter, and said unto Jesus, Lord, it is good for us to be here: if thou wilt, let us make here three tabernacles; one for thee, and one for Moses, and one for Elias.[5] While he yet spake, behold, a bright cloud overshadowed them: and behold a voice out of the cloud, which said, This is my beloved Son, in whom I am well pleased; hear ye him.[6] And when the disciples heard it, they fell on their face, and were sore afraid.[7] And Jesus came and touched them, and said, Arise, and be not afraid.[8] *And when they had lifted up their eyes, they saw no man, save Jesus only.*[9] *And as they came down from the mountain, Jesus charged them, saying, Tell the vision to no man, until the Son of man be risen again from the dead.*

Out of the twelve disciples Jesus had three transformational thinkers. Peter, James and John were chosen from among the Twelve to follow Jesus where the others were not allowed to go. Matthew 17:1, says after six days Jesus took Peter, James and John and brought them up into a high mountain apart. The indications are that he separated them from the rest of the group, to expose them to something that the rest of the group would not experience. Consequently, they would learn what the other nine would not, and know what the other nine would not know. I am convinced that transformational thinkers often see, learn and know what others do not and consequently, may have a perspective that those without that exposure will not have, and may consider foolish, illogical and even unspiritual.

Using this paradigm of Christ with Peter, James and John, we might conclude that only 25% of those who walk with us are transformational thinkers. We know that these three were transformational thinkers, because they saw Jesus transformed or transfigured. To understand this releases transformational leaders to prepare lessons for the smaller group that are key and significant to their callings and purpose, which are different from their dealings with the rest. Leaders are often vulnerable to lose many of their greatest thinkers when they are distracted by the needs of the 75%, the masses, who are content to live in a survival mode. Their smaller constituents are beyond that needs-driven modality. They are frustrated and often leave settings where only their basic needs are being addressed, in search of much more.

Verse 2 of Matthew 17 reveals that the transfiguration/transformation showed them the future glorification of the Resurrected Christ even though he had not died yet. They were able to see beyond their current reality. Acquiring a vision or a preview of the future brings those who are allowed to see it, into a greater measure of faith, hope and determination. This revelation became their now faith and substance of things hoped for! Peter, James and John were blessed with that exposure. They were selected for this special assignment. The others were left behind while these three were called to go with Him, up in a high mountain. In the Bible, mountains are symbols of places of revelation. The "high" mountain then would speak of a place of "great' revelation, where what they will see is greater than what they have ever seen. As a matter of fact, this experience would not be repeated. He could not ask those who think in terms of 'business as usual' to go to a place that is 'unusual.' If you are going into a supernatural place you need to be able to supernaturally relate. The text even uses the term "apart," as if to be intentional about the fact that others would not, and could not be part of this experience; not even accidentally exposed.

The 7th Day

Matthew 17:1 states, "After six days" he taketh Peter, James and John. We are in the "after six days" timeframe. Symbolically, six is the number of man. Man was created on the sixth day. "After six days" would indicate, after the time of the efforts of men. After "six days" comes the 'seventh day." The seventh day, prophetically, is the day we are currently living in. Seven is a number that we often refer to when we speak of God resting; thus it is the day of the Lord. The apostle, Peter says (II Peter 3:8) that, *"one day is with the Lord as a thousand years, and a thousand years as one day."* Using Peter's mathematic calculation and the chronology that the Bible gives us from Genesis until now, we can conclude that there has been a lapse of seven thousand years, which calculates as seven days. There is thousand years from Adam to Abraham (equivalent to two days). There are two thousand more years from Abraham to Jesus (equivalent to two more days). Then there has been two thousand years from Jesus to year 2000 AD (equivalent to two days). This gives us the six complete days, which brings us into the seventh day, beginning approximately in year 2000, or in the twenty first century. This places us in the 7th day of God, or seven thousand years since creation. In the 7th day, the Lord takes the transformational thinker up into a high mountain. In this place, He provides the believer the opportunity to know and encounter Him in a manner in which he has never known Him before. However, this type of encounter requires a change in thinking and a surrendering of one's mind to the Lord. The masses will not ascend to the high place because they cannot ascertain this place under natural propensities; He takes them and brings them up.

Our goal should be to ascend. We and those connected to us may not arrive in this place at the same time, but there is no need for alarm. The opportunity is available to them also. Each of us must have an individual experience and recognize that our encounters are unique and what was given to me may not be given to another. Peter, James and John beheld His transfiguration and it changed their thinking and their perspective.

When our thinking is transformed, we can take no thought for what we are going to eat or drink. We cannot be consumed by those basic needs. We have to transcend beyond that. When my boys were growing up they were not concerned about money. When it was time to eat, they just ordered whatever they wanted. They had no concerns. They knew their father would provide. When we ascend beyond this place, we will find ourselves in the ultimate place with God where we can dream and embrace the impossible. Transformational thinkers seek first the kingdom of God and his righteousness, and all other things are added (Matthew 6:33). This allows the transformational thinker to ascend and transcend thoughts of needs, housing, food and clothing, knowing that God has promised to provide these natural needs. This often leads to promotion in lifestyle and freedom from health related issues.

Transformational Thinkers and the World around Us

Promotions will not just come from within the nuclear church, but from the extended church as well, which will posture and position us to take the kingdoms of this world. We are on the brink of a spiritual revolution headed by those who are in a place of transformational thinking. These revolutionaries will bring God's rule and reign to bear in places that have been dominated and devastated by the evil powers of darkness. The saints who are transformational thinkers are coming forth with great power and authority to affect the entire world, including the church. The move is prophetic and powerful, and it will prepare the way of the Lord before His return. According to the Scripture, Jesus will sit at God's right hand until all of His enemies are put under His feet (Hebrews 10:13). This massive movement of revolutionaries is not coming to take sides, but to take over.

The revolution will take us into our promised land. Our promised land is the nations and every kingdom of this world. Manna is about to cease as we move from wilderness provisions to the abundance of God's promise. As the Lord brings the transformational thinkers into the Promised Land, we will encounter seven kingdoms (nations) of the world "greater and mightier" than us according to Deuteronomy 7:1. Joshua's enemies were the Hittites, Girgashites, Amorites, Canaanites, Perizzites, Hivites and Jebusites. For us, these nations represent seven spirits of the seven nations that occupy mountains that shape society: media, government, education, economy, religion, art/entertainment/celebration and family. The kingdoms of this world must become the kingdoms of our Lord and His Christ, where he shall reign forever and ever (Revelations 11:15).

Apostles, prophets, evangelists, pastors and teachers who walk in the fullness of Christ's anointing are engaging in the perfecting of the saints for the work of ministry and the edification of the saints (Ephesians 4:11-12). These saints will infiltrate the societal strongholds and advance the kingdom of the Lord, our God. This places a great sense of urgency on spiritual leaders today, to develop transformational thinkers both for the local church and the marketplace. The grace that Christ gives the believer, which I call God's enabling ability, is effective and efficient wherever the need to capitalize on it occurs. So as a transformational leader, I am preparing transformational thinkers to enter into government, religion, business, entertainment, media, family, and education. Though church titles are not transferrable into the marketplace, the grace gifts are. Even now, God is strategically placing apostles, prophets, evangelists, pastors and teachers throughout the kingdoms of this world. Their placement, their strategies, their tactics and successes are being orchestrated by the plan of God for His earth.

Transformational Thinkers and Key Assignments

When we are blessed by the Lord to witness transformation, as Peter, James and John were, we are really being prepared for future assignments that others who have not witnessed transformation, cannot handle. This becomes quite evident when the three who are taken up in the high mountain are also the three who are invited to go with Him into the Garden of Gethsemane, as He prepares to be betrayed, tried and crucified. Receiving a preview of Christ's future glory prepared them in a different matter to partake and bear witness of His sufferings and agony in the Garden. Because they had witnessed His ultimate outcome in the spirit realm, they were best qualified to retain their faith and to cover Him in prayer as He experienced the trauma of the warfare between His spirit, soul and body. Though they failed at remaining alert and fervent in prayer, their transformational experience on the mountain was now augmented by another transformational experience in the Garden.

Mind Renewal

Jeremiah 29:11 in the Message Bible says, "*I know what I am doing. I have it all planned out-- plans to take care of you, not to abandon you, plans to give you the future you hope for.*" In Romans 12:1-3, there is a denotation that transformation comes through your thinking. It says that you are going to be transformed by the renewing of your mind. We often look for transformation to change our thinking, but it says the renewing of your mind births you into a place of transformation. We must do it so we can prove God's good, acceptable and perfect will. Verse 3 says, "*For I say through the grace given unto me that every man that is among you is to not think of himself more highly than he ought to think; but to think soberly, according as God has dealt to every man the measure of faith.*" Sobriety is relative; it is not an absolute. One man's drunkenness is another man's sobriety. The Bible says think of yourself soberly which is determined by our measure of faith.

Faith drives sobriety. Your measure of faith determines how you see yourself and how you think. Faith affords us the opportunity to reach a higher place. We cannot always share how we think because it may be intoxicating to others. Our faith allows us to build foundations in places where others may not be allowed. Through faith, we gain admission to this place on an ongoing basis. You may have never thought that this place was accessible to you, but the Lord is bringing you into this place. You are moving forward and with every step you are getting closer to Him.

Transformational thinkers are examples to others. There are six areas in particular in which they must guide others:

1) In Word - Transformational thinkers teach sound doctrine.
2) In Conversation - Transformational thinkers engage in discourse that is edifying and reflective of a transformed mind.
3) In Charity - Transformational thinkers are patient, kind, generous, humble, courteous, unselfish, good tempered, righteous and sincere.
4) In Spirit - Transformational thinkers are led by the Spirit and engage in spiritual worship
5) In Faith - Transformational thinkers are full of faith
6) In Purity - Transformational thinkers are holy and lead pure lives.

Chapter 6

Identifying the Plan of God for Your Life

Many people blame those around them for their lot in life. In transformational thinking, people learn that we can be champions of change, if we recognize that it is the choices that we make that determine the direction of our lives. In this regard, we have to learn how to make better decisions more often in order to improve our lives. When we realize that our best thinking propelled us into where we are today, we have little choice but to choose more carefully. It is an inside-out process of change that starts with a personal inventory of defining who we are and where we want to go. This then extends outwards to others.

If you know that this is your time, you should declare it. There is not a devil in hell that can rob you of this moment. Whatever has happened to you up to this point has happened for a purpose. Even the experiences that we classify as 'bad' have a way of being transforming. Roman 8:28 declares that all things point to purpose. I learned to stop despising my experiences no matter how grotesque because all things are purposed. When we allow whatever the experience may be, to change our way of thinking, and transform our perspectives, we are better equipped to move forward and upward.

Transfiguration effects change for a process by which something becomes what it was created to be. This deals with the creative purpose for why a person, place or thing exists. It comes about gradually, by metamorphosis; these changes happen in stages. Transfiguration implies an intended process, not just happening by happen stance. Thus, it is a deliberate process, which I believe is orchestrated and ordained by God, to bring us in alignment to why we are here. It is amidst the metamorphosis that I begin to see who I am, why I exist, and what I am supposed to be doing.

God wants your process to continue. Stop squirming like a worm; endure the process. Transfiguration denotes that there is a transformation or a radical change that comes from within; it cannot be stimulated from the outside. Since these processes were not triggered by us, we cannot stop them. God's efforts transcend the efforts of men. If men are the source of where you originate and where you are going, when they are not pleased with you, they will stop it. Some people get a thrill out of dominating and intimidating you.

I do not want a God that is not sure about my destiny, making up his mind while I am in route, but I need a God who has known me before the foundation of the world (Romans 8: 29, 30). He alone knows every detail of His plan for us. So we trust Him, and take solace in knowing that, 'that is good for the saints which does their souls good.' Every providence aligns itself and tends to the spiritual good of those that love God. Transformation is realized as these experiences break us off from sin, bringing us nearer to God, weaning us from the world, and fitting us for heaven. Transformational thinkers have a peace from within when we are corrected for acting out of character, bringing us back to where we belong. Nothing in our lives is a surprise to God, for *"whom he did foreknow, he also did predestinate to be conformed to the image of his Son"* (Romans 8: 29-30). In God's original design for man, everything was included that would bring the Father glory and honor from the man He created. Grace has made available to each of us, through Jesus Christ, all things that pertain to life and godliness.

God's Plan for Us

To have a clear understanding of what God's purpose is for us would certainly change our whole outlook on life and our commitment to God's service. Our life would take on a whole new dimension – transformational.

Paul, in writing to the Ephesians, starts not with the fall of man, but with the "Eternal Father." And, he states that God's purpose began "before the foundation of the world." Paul goes on to teach that God's purpose for the entire universe is to be realized through, and centering in, His Son, Jesus Christ.

To get a grasp of God's eternal purpose, spoken of by Paul, we must realize that it was determined in God's heart, not because man sinned, but before the world was made.

"Paul, an apostle of Christ Jesus by the will of God, To the saints in Ephesus, the faithful in Christ Jesus: Grace and peace to you from God our Father and the Lord Jesus Christ.[speaking to born-again saints] Praise be to the God and Father of our Lord Jesus Christ, who has blessed us in the heavenly realms with every spiritual blessing in Christ! For He [God, the Father] chose us in Him [Jesus Christ] before the creation of the world to be holy and blameless in his sight. In love He predestined us to be adopted as His sons through Jesus Christ, in

accordance with His pleasure and will - to the praise of His glorious grace, which He [Father] has freely given us in the One He loves." Ephesians 1:1-6 NIV

To embrace the thought that each of us was in the purpose that was in the Father's heart before the foundation of the world is a transforming. This truth can radically change our lives. The fellowship between God, the Father, and His Son, Jesus Christ, and the Holy Spirit in eternity past was so prized, so amazing, that God desired to have many sons conformed to the image of His Son. With great anticipation, God planned that His "eternal Son" would become the incarnate Son, robed in flesh, and sharing His vital life with the human family, yet to be created! God planned to visit earth by the incarnation of His Son, not because man sinned, but in order for Jesus to take on the very life of man.

Paul does point out in verse 7 that because man would sin, he needed redemption and this provision was also in Christ Jesus. He writes, *"In Him [in Christ Jesus] we have redemption through His blood, the forgiveness of sins, in accordance with the riches of God's grace."*

Verses 8-10 continue, *"He lavished on us with all wisdom and understanding. And He made known to us the mystery of His will according to His good pleasure, which He purposed in Christ, {10} to be put into effect when the times will have reached their fulfillment--to bring all things in heaven and on earth together under one head, even Christ."*

This is a transformational fact that, God, the Father, determined that His Son should become incarnate as the means of bringing a vast family of sons into the glorious measure of full stature. Paul was looking at God's eternal purpose for man, while he was "seated with Him in heavenly places." Things certainly look different when viewing the whole picture from the veranda of the universe. Paul sees the eternal Father yearning for a vast family of sons conformed to the image of the eternal Son, in whom He found such delight.

This Time of Transformation for the Church

Looking at Ephesians 3:10-11, we read, *"His intent [God's intent] was that now [in this day and age] through the church, the manifold wisdom of God should be made known to the rulers and authorities in the heavenly realms, according to His eternal purpose which He accomplished in Christ Jesus or Lord."* Phillips Translation renders verse 11, *"To the powers and authorities in the heavenly realm God, by the Church, display the innumerable aspects of God's wisdom."*

God's eternal purpose and intent is to display to the entire universe, for all of eternity, His matchless wisdom by conforming "many sons" into the image of His own dear Son, Jesus Christ.

When God created man and placed him on earth, man was created in innocence. God's plan and eternal purpose was to share His life with man and to bring him to perfection-- spiritual maturity. It was not man's sin (or, defection) that determined this purpose of God sharing His life, but rather, it was in the Father's original planning. Before man was ever created, before he ever sinned, God determined to share His life through His Son. If we can embrace the fact that there is a bigger picture than just the one we see, we can better understand that every experience and occurrence that life offers is part of a transformation plan that is working to reveal His will to us.

Soulish or Spiritual Transformation

By "soulish," I am referring to man living only by the powers of his soul – his mind, will and emotions.

While, it is true that before there can be true spiritual transformation, there must be a radical deliverance [this is salvation]. However, this deliverance is only the doorway to spiritual development. Do not get so interested in the fact of being "free from sin" or, "just making it to heaven," that it warps you into lethargy. Do not let escape from sin and its penalty become your only goal. God helps us to see that His eternal purpose is to develop us into full stature.

Many merely want God to deliver them from all troubles, to grant them an easier life. They are controlled by a philosophy of "escapism." These are the 75% that I spoke of in an earlier chapter. They are not as Scripture teaches, *"dead indeed unto our old selfish nature,"* and, that we *"must be alive to God."*

Paul, with all his problems, did not once write with self-pity. Never once did he speak of "escapism." He never pleaded with the Church to pray on his behalf that God make his life easier, but, rather, he was gripped with one concept, stated in Philippians 1:12, *"that all things that happen to me might work for the furtherance of the Gospel."*

If you have had a narrow perspective of "escapism," you are not a transformational thinker! Our prayer should be that God would enable us to see His original plan and dedicate us to His purpose. Jesus made a way of escaping and conquering. He set us free from sin, self, the world and Satan. For too long many have been held in bondage by these monarchs, not realizing that their tyranny has been broken. Jesus died and rose for our escape, but God's purpose is far more than that. Do not stop at just a way of escape. The cross and resurrection is the way of fulfillment. What God offered Adam in the Garden of Eden, Adam dodged, now God presents the same offer to you and me.

2 Timothy 1:8 (Phillips Translation) states, *"Accept, as I do, all the hardships that faithfulness the Gospel entails, in the strength that God gives you. For He has rescued us from all that is really evil, AND called us to a life of holiness, not because of any of our achievement, but for HIS OWN PURPOSE."* (emphasis is mine)

How characteristic of Paul to go back to God's eternal viewpoint. He does not start with man's fallen condition, but, rather he starts with the Father's original purpose before time began. That's transformational!

Verses 9-10 continues, *"Before time began God planned to give us in Christ the grace to achieve this purpose but it is only since our Savior Jesus Christ has been revealed that the method has become apparent."*

It is possible to be saved from destruction and yet lost to the ultimate intention which God has in mind. That is often the case with those who refuse, resist or avoid the power of transformational thinking, by not taking on the mind of Christ.

Chapter 7

Moving Into a Place Beyond

There is a tremendous move in religion to make all religions equal in order to remove conflict, but God has always proved himself through conflict. In our desire not to be contrary, we have taken on the spirit of the world. In a desire not to get stuck in *old time holiness,* we have forgotten how to live righteously. Consequently, there is a measure of carnality that the church has become tolerant of and we have not asked the Lord to cleanse us of it. I believe you can be successful and holy without compromising the righteousness of God. We have to get rid of this carnality. Carnality breeds mediocrity. Mediocrity breeds stagnation and compromise. Mediocrity by definition means: *average, moderate, or common.* The Christ in us should make us above average every day. Whatever we do as Christians, we must do it with excellence. We cannot afford to compromise and settle for less.

God designed us to be limitless in our thinking and in our accomplishments; however, something in us finds satisfaction in achieving even at the very basic levels. Even though our humanity finds satisfaction in mediocrity, there's a more righteous part of us that desires to tap into the One who created us and who provokes us to reach for the impossible. When He created us He pulled us from His omnipotent self. We are derivatives of an omnipotent God. He made us in His likeness and image and He transferred to us His own potential. The word *potential* is not in the Bible, but the Bible is full of inferences that talk about one's ability and capability. Genesis 1 reveals how He designed us, God created us in His image, male and female He created them. We came out of God and we are His dwelling place. He is not diminished by living inside of us. He is still all God. He designed us to be a limitless people that are only limited by God not our own intellect, someone else's opinion, or an environment. We must go beyond our best and find the better than best. What could we accomplish if we transformed our thinking and tapped into the omnipotence, omniscience, omnipresence of God living inside of us?

When we connect, through our faith, to Jesus, He empowers us to return to our original mode of operation—how He created us to be, just like Him. If we are not like Him, we need to make it our goal. The earth was not created to subdue or handicap man's potential. He made us to have dominion over the earth. We have to take the authority that has been given to us to control the earth. God thinks in terms of potential. He is not excited about what you have already done—that is old and in the past—what can you do better today? God designed us to think on things that have not yet manifested.

In Philippians 3:13, 14 (NIV) Paul declares, *"Brothers and sisters, I do not consider myself yet to have taken hold of it. But one thing I do: Forgetting what is behind and straining toward what is ahead, I press on toward the goal to win the prize for which God has called me heavenward in Christ Jesus."* We like to ascribe these verses to negative situations in our lives, but what would these verses mean for our lives if we believed He was also talking about those things that we considered good. The text would then imply that we have not done all that we can do and what we have done we can do better. God wants us to forget things that worked before but that were not the optimum. God wants us to get more accomplished this year than we accomplished last year. If this year looks the same as last year, then our faith has not grown and our thinking has not been transformed. We must not be mediocre in our natural or spiritual pursuits.

We must continue to genuinely hunger and thirst for the Lord so that we may continue to be enlarged spiritually. What we get of Him spiritually grows our capacity for Him and results in a different kind of desire of Him.

We must dare to be segregationist. A spiritual segregationist serves the only true and living God. There is no room for religious tolerance, and no religious utopia. We must aggressively progress from a place of visitation, through a place of demonstration, to a dwelling place of habitation. The tabernacle of Moses provides an excellent model in which to display this idea when we observe that the Outer Court was a place that the people visited to bring their sacrifices. The Holy Place was a court where man used sacred items to demonstrate the power and presence of God. Lastly, the Most Holy Place was where God lives; beyond the veil.

A Place of Visitation

The Outer Court in the tabernacle of Moses can also be seen as the first dimension of God. It is a place of visitation where God either received or rejected the sacrifices that were offered for the people. In the outer court, there was the brazen altar which was made of wood and brass. The brazen altar was a bloody place. Here the blood of the sacrifices stained the altar. Wood is symbolic of humanity. Brass represents judgment. This was the place where man made an effort to satisfy the judgment of God and find His favor.

A Place of Demonstration

In the Inner Court or Holy Place, the second dimension or section of the Tabernacle, there was the table of shew bread. The unleavened bread was placed there every Sabbath and eaten by the priest. The bread speaks of Christ as the bread of life. Also in this court was the golden altar of incense which symbolizes the intercessory prayer of the saints. The final piece of furniture was the golden lampstand that represents Christ, the light of the world. All of these items were made of wood overlaid with gold, which symbolizes God working with man to make Him known.

Outer Court	Inner Court	Holy of Holies
Visitation	Demonstration	Habitation
Way	Truth	Life
Door	Gate	Veil
Chosen -called	Servants	Friends
World	Church	Kingdom
Body	Soul	Spirit
Power	Might	Spirit
Oxen	Sheep	Dove
Father	Son	Holy Spirit
Savior	King	Lord
Called	Justified	Glorified
Good	Acceptable	Perfect

The demonstration or manifestation in this court requires the involvement of God and man. In the inner court, there was no bread unless man baked it; no burning incense except the priest lit it; and no oil unless a man poured it. Now, because of the finished work of Christ, every believer gets involved in the work of Christ, and making Him known. We feed off of His word as the bread of life. We pray and intercede unto the Lord anytime and anywhere. Our prayers become a sweet smelling odor in the nostrils of God. We also are vessels through whom the oil of the Spirit flows. We are the light of the world.

A Place of Habitation

In the Holy of Holies, or the third dimension of God, is the dwelling place of the spirit of God. Everything in the Holy of Holies is made with beaten gold, which speaks of nothing but God; man is not involved. This is all about God. However, man must pass through the veil to experience the presence of God. The High Priest made it behind the veil once a year on the Day of Atonement, to sprinkle blood on the Mercy Seat, for atonement of the sins of men. This visit was well orchestrated, as the High Priest had to be careful not to offend God, with his own unrighteousness. Thus, a rope with bells and pomegranates was tied to his ankle, so that if He was judged and died behind the veil, and the bells stopped ringing and he would be pulled out by the rope.

The New Testament Anti-Type

The Lord in his sovereignty has a pattern already set for us in the Tabernacle of how the New Testament believer would come to Christ.

We must come through the gate, the door, and the veil. John 14:6 says, *"Jesus said unto him, I am the way, the truth, and the life: no man cometh unto the Father, but by me."* The Gate to the Outer Court was known as the "way." The Door to the Holy place was known as the "truth." The Veil that led to the Most Holy Place was known as the "life." Jesus was then saying that He is the only pathway or approach to God. Let us examine the Scriptures as it relates to the tabernacle and other patterns set forth in God's word.

In Matthew 16:13-16, *"When Jesus came into the coasts of Caesarea Philippi, he asked the disciples, saying, Who do men say that I the Son of man am? And they said, some say that thou art John the Baptist: some, Elias; and others, Jeremias, or one of the prophets. He saith unto them, But who say ye that I am? And Simon Peter answered and said, Thou art the Christ, the Son of the living God."* (KJV) Because of this revelation, from the right source-the Father, Peter was given a revelation of himself and another level of spiritual responsibility. The Church of the Living God has assumed this assignment. Christ builds the church and gives the Church keys to the kingdom. Additionally, the Church has powers to bind and loose. What we need is a revelation of truth revealed by the Holy Spirit of how to take the kingdom by force.

In Revelation 1:9, John indicates that it was *"...the Lord's day,"* a day of rest, when he received the great revelation on the Isle of Patmos. He was in a place of resting on the Sabbath of the Lord when he admonished us to cease from our labor. In this same verse, a distinct sound is heard, one voice as clear as a trumpet.

Verse 12 indicates to us that the voice that John heard could not have been heard in a regular position, but he needed to see, so he turned to see and to get a working perception. What John saw later in verse 13 were seven golden candlesticks, which are found in the second dimension of the Tabernacle. This is the dimension of the church, the inner court, the demonstration. He was not turning *in* the church, but he was turning *to* the church. John was in a dimension beyond the church, the place beyond the veil, the dimension of the kingdom.

Ezekiel's vision (Ezekiel 47) shows a river flowing out southward into the salt sea, out of the corner of the east gate. He saw one existing dimension. There was no veil and the glory of God could be clearly seen. The veil only disappears when there is a renting of it- the flesh. The flesh has an opinion and a mindset of its own. The flesh is carnality. The carnal believer wants a combination of milk and meat. The mature believer in Christ only desires strong meat. In the place of habitation, you are no longer fighting the will of God for your life, but you are totally surrendered.

This entire chapter speaks to those who are open and objective in their pursuit of God and will allow their thinking to be affected by a revelation of Christ in the Old and New Testaments. Revelation requires manifestation. When God exposes himself to man, there is a spiritual responsibility. That is what Peter and John received after their revelations. We need men and women in the Body today who are available to see and hear from God those things that others are unable to receive. A radical revelation will produce a radical thinker, who will do great exploits in the Kingdom.

Chapter 8

Wrong Thinking

Romans 12:1-3 *"Therefore, I urge you, brothers and sisters, in view of God's mercy, to offer your bodies as a living sacrifice, holy and pleasing to God—this is your true and proper worship. ² Do not conform to the pattern of this world, but be transformed by the renewing of your mind. Then you will be able to test and approve what God's will is—his good, pleasing and perfect will. ³ For by the grace given me I say to every one of you: Do not think of yourself more highly than you ought, but rather think of yourself with sober judgment, in accordance with the faith God has distributed to each of you."*

Philippians 4:8 *"Finally, brothers and sisters, whatever is true, whatever is noble, whatever is right, whatever is pure, whatever is lovely, whatever is admirable—if anything is excellent or praiseworthy—think about such things."*

Psalm 13:2 *"How long must I wrestle with my thoughts and day after day have sorrow in my heart? How long will my enemy triumph over me?"*

Psalm 139:23 *"Search me, God, and know my heart; test me and know my anxious thoughts."*

Isaiah 55:8-9 *"For my thoughts are not your thoughts, neither are your ways my ways," declares the Lord. As the heavens are higher than the earth, so are my ways higher than your ways and my thoughts than your thoughts."*

Individuals that are convicted of capital crimes are often given a life sentence. We know this to be a life lived imprisoned by a monotonous routine without the possibility of release. The sentence reduces the convicted to a zombie like state of mind. When we think of a prison, we think of high stone walls, razor wire and guard towers that house the incorrigible. But the worst kind of prison is the kind we build within ourselves- the feeling of being trapped by our perceived limitations; dreading getting up to go to the same job, driving the same route, working with the same people and being overwhelmed by debt that influences every decision we make. I know many people who may not wear an orange jump suit with a number on it, but are clothed in an attitude of apathy and passivity because of the prison they have built over the years between their ears.

Many believers look forward to the hope of life after death while never really understanding that there is life after birth. Life as Jesus intended it is not a life sentence with the greatest days being the day you were born again and awaiting the day of your release via the rapture. Too many simply endure and never enjoy the journey called life. Jesus said *the thief comes to kill, steal and to destroy but I am come that you might have life and have it more abundantly*! (John 10:10) Who or what is the thief that steals this abundant life that is our inheritance? I believe the thief is simply wrong thinking, or a wrong mindset. The hinges of the door of this inner prison that we have created can swing open when we identify the thief. The worst threat in life is not death, but that we die without every really knowing how to live. Ironically, studies show that people have a far greater fear of living than they do of dying.

Webster defines *thinking* as the action of using your mind to produce ideas, decisions, memories; the activity of thinking about something; forming an opinion or judgment; a way of thinking that is characteristic of a particular group, time period, etc.

Thought can refer to the ideas or arrangements of ideas that result from thinking, the act of producing thoughts, or the process of producing thoughts. Although thought is a fundamental human activity familiar to everyone, there is no generally accepted agreement as to what thought is or how it is created. Thoughts are the result or product of either spontaneous or willed acts of thinking.

Because thought underlies many human actions and interactions, understanding its physical and metaphysical origins, processes, and effects has been a longstanding goal of many academic disciplines including psychology, neuroscience, philosophy, artificial intelligence, biology, sociology and cognitive science.

It is generally accepted that thinking allows humans to make sense of, interpret, represent or model the world they experience, and to make predictions about that world. This equates to effective living as these persons then engage in strategies and plans to accomplish those goals.

Habitual Thinking - Worry

It may seem strange at this point to turn to the subject of worry. However, worry is the antitheses of passion. Worry drains us of energy and enthusiasm leaving us emotionally anemic. Jesus describes the effects of worry in Matthew 6:31; *"Therefore take no thought saying what shall we eat? Or what shall we drink? Or wherewithal shall we be clothed?"* Even though the word worry is not used in this passage, it is implied by the word "thought." This is a kind of habitual thinking; the kind of mental mazes we get into by always thinking of problems rather than possibilities.

Our culture is very familiar with obsessive disorders that cripple even the most gifted individuals. These mental mazes have resulted in the loss of income and quality of life. Mark 4:19, *"The cares of this world and the deceitfulness of riches and the lusts of other things entering in choke the word and it becomes unfruitful."* The word *worry* literally means to choke or suffocate. We should live inspired lives. Inspiration or being inspired is God breathing in us and through us. Worry, on the contrary, asphyxiates the passion we should be breathing.

As adults, we envy the undaunted enthusiasm and energy of children bubbling over with a passion for life. Unlike us, they have not been introduced to worry. I remember, when my sons were children, hearing them from the back seat of the car yelling, "Look dad, look!" Only to discover that they were seeing for the first time something that was common place to me. They lived in wonderment; while I lived in worry.

We were children that matured, got married and got a mortgage. As children, my sons never expressed a concern over whether or not our bills were paid. They never gave one thought to how much money it took to pay our mortgage or to put food on the table. They trusted in my ability to provide. When we worry over these things, we fail to remember that if we, being evil, know how to give good things to our children how much more will the heavenly Father give good things to them that ask. Our asking has to be in line with His will and we embrace His will as we transform our thinking.

Thinking Errors

What you believe is very powerful. If you have toxic emotions of fear, guilt and depression, it is because you have wrong thinking, and you have wrong thinking because of wrong believing. Wrong thinking leads to wrong behavior. To avoid wrong behavior, we should perhaps begin by being sensitive to thinking errors. Thinking errors are "mistakes" in the way someone thinks. Thinking errors let a person blame other people or situations for his/her wrong doing.

For clarity, let me give you seven (7) thinking errors (adapted from family therapist Kim Molnar)[4] that we use to avoid responsibility and accountability for our wrong behaviors

1. Justifying – finding reason for what we have done.
2. Blame – finding fault in another person, and attempting to put responsibility for our own behavior on others. We find someone or something else to be responsible.

---

[4] http://www.kmolnar.com/Thinking_Errors.html

3. Excuse Making – avoiding accountability for one's own actions by blaming situations or things for our own behavior.
4. Hop-overs – avoiding responsibility by avoiding the issue, and shifting the focus to someone or changing the topic to something else.
5. Lying – being deceptive and dishonest by falsification or altering the facts. This can be done by:
   a. Omission – telling only partial truths.
   b. Commission – denying the truth or saying something is true when it's not.
   c. Assent – faking agreement to expedite the resolve of the conflict; avoiding combat.
6. Anger – becoming angry in order to get the focus off of our inappropriate behavior and on to the anger, causing people to focus on calming us down or leaving others alone.
7. Minimizing – making the problem seem smaller so that we can avoid being accountable for our behaviors.

When these practices have been part of our lives and behavior for long periods of time, there must be aggressive intervention in our lives to transform our thinking. I would suggest the need for a supernatural encounter that changes and renews our mindsets.

Conforming versus Transforming

The Holy Spirit can change the way you think. When your thinking changes, your life changes. Life is greatly affected by how you think. If you think you can, you will. Romans 12:1-3 (NIV) states, *"Do not conform to the pattern of this world, but be transformed by the renewing of your mind*." This verse contrasts conforming to transforming. The text admonishes us to not conform to the world. We cannot allow the world to pressure us to become like it. We cannot look like it looks or sound like it sounds. We will experience transformation as our mind is renewed. The renewing of the mind is an ongoing experience it is not a single act. It is not something that we force ourselves to do; it is something that we should desire. As we yield to the transforming of our mind, we submit to the Lord's perfect will for our lives. Romans 12: 2b implies that then you will be able to test and approve what God's will is—His good, pleasing and perfect will.

There is a progression in good, acceptable and perfect. When we first accept Christ, it is impossible for us to live out His perfect will because we have not learned to trust Him like that. The perfect will comes about as we lose our identities and the Christ of the Bible becomes the Christ of our lives. When one first gets saved he does well to do His good will. He moves from the good to the acceptable as he matures in Him and the Lord says, "I accept that." It is not perfect, but He accepts it. David said he would not offer to the Lord something that has cost him nothing. (II Samuel 24:24). A real sacrifice will cost you something, but it will not kill you; it brings life. This is the paradigm shift from the old to the new. In the old, the sacrifice must die; however, in the new, the sacrifice must live. It is a privilege to be a living sacrifice. We give Him our all, but it does not cost us everything. It is a spiritual act of worship that results in the transforming of our thinking.

When we take on the fullness of Christ, we walk in the perfect will of God. You and I alone cannot perfectly satisfy God. We do not have the ability. We are not that righteous, smart or holy. The perfect will of God is fulfilled in us as we take on Christ. We have the propensity to get comfortable and relax after we have declared ourselves righteous.

Wrong Thinking

The church is full of people who are ready for heaven but not earth. Every believer has to make a conscious decision to daily give himself to the Lord.

Romans 12:3 says *"do not think of yourself more highly than you ought."* He wants us to think highly, but not more highly than we ought. Sometimes we struggle with how we think of ourselves. Sometimes it is a challenge to think of ourselves highly at all. Some people do not have a proper perspective. We have to remember that we are somebody for the Lord has redeemed us. We can think highly of ourselves, but likewise we have to be balanced- displaying sober judgment. Think of this in accordance to the measure of faith that God has given each of us. Sobriety is determined by the measure of faith that God has given. Transformational thinkers think according to their faith. Everyone has been given a measure of faith. The problem is that some believers have not grown beyond a cup and they cannot understand why others have megatons of faith.

I am concerned that some people do not experience the fullness of God because they are limited by their own ways and resources. God can do so much more than we can ask or think. There is a measure of God's ability to bless, provide, and secure us beyond where we are now. We must be transformed by the renewing of the minds, thus taking our limits off of God, and allowing Him to be fully God.

The root word of conform and transform is *form*. The difference between conforming and transforming is our performing. I am having a difficult time building the bridge of performing that gets me from conforming to transforming. I am trying to perform until I am transformed by the renewing of my mind. Who am I? We must consider our formation. Who am I becoming? What is my role? What is God's role?

The question has always been: How do believers engage the world? My generation grew up under the doctrine of separation. We were told that there should be no relationship between the saints and the world. We later realized that separation does not work if you want to win the world. Today, the church has set aside the doctrine of separation and has developed other models: identification, transformational and incarnational. The doctrine of identification says go among unbelievers. However, there is a risk involved if the believer's light is overpowered by the unbeliever's darkness.

Like the identification model, the transformational model requires engagement in the world; however, it goes beyond the identification model in that it espouses the truth that the believer can cause those they encounter to change. Yet, like identification, there is also a danger in that because the situations can be so perplexing that the believer can become victimized by the same problems.

Incarnational is the last model. John 1 says the Word was made flesh and we beheld him as the only begotten of the Father full of grace and truth. Jesus is our model. We have come into the word as flesh, but we live our lives as the word of God. The flesh is being made the word. I am God moving in the earth. As he is so are we in the world.

As transformational thinkers, we must embrace this truth. *"As He is in the world, so are we"* I John 4:17. We have the ability to think the way He thinks. A few years ago, WWJD- *"What would Jesus do?"* was a mega marketing scheme. Everyone was saying it or displaying it via bracelets, tee shirts etc. It caused even the unrighteous to pause and think. It made even those who did not believe in His deity, but just thought He was "nice", to stop and think-- How did he do it? He functioned under a greater law. He did only what the Father said.

Chapter 9

Prophetic Imagination

There is a close relationship between how we think and what we can imagine. Did you know that the Holy Spirit uses your imagination to prophecy your future? Jesus taught that all things are possible to him that believeth (Mark 9:23, KJV). Can you see yourself walking out the promises of God for your life? Can you see yourself living in victory? Can you believe that people who have transformed their thinking can live their lives according to the perfect will of God?

God created us with a unique ability to see prophetic possibilities. The capacity to see in this manner is called your "imagination."

When I start to think of the unseen from my imagination, I tap into my God ability to imagine or think like God imagines or thinks. My ability to imagine comes out of the root word "image." His image gives me the ability to imagine like God imagines. When I believe the imagination is real, then suddenly I start to see myself beyond the limitations. When I engage my prophetic imagination, I start to think outside of the wall that is before me and suddenly I do not see the wall. I see myself on the other side because God has given me strategies that are from Him. It is not me.

Imaginations create images for your future. To understand prophetic imaginations is to understand God's design for His sons and daughters. God created you as a Spirit-led believer not just as a Spirit-born believer. As you harness the power of prophetic imagination you can enter the realm of "all things possible" and change your life! Prophetic imaginations cause you to see life differently. As a believer, you have the mind of Christ and the ability to control your imaginations. As a result, you can devise positive and attainable goals. As a born again believer, you have the power to change your world. Our lives have been shaped by the imaginations of others. From the clothes we wear to the cars we drive, we have been subject to someone's imagination. Psalms 139:14 says that we are fearfully and wonderfully made. Our ability to imagine comes from Him.

Every great achievement starts within the imagination of man. Again, Jesus said, "All things are possible to him that believeth." Do you know that everything starts with a thought, dream, vision, imagination or image? Every improvement in the world has been the result of someone imagining something better. God designed us with the power of prophetic imagination. A prophetic imagination allows us to become seers. We become like Samuel, Gad and Asaph who saw God's will and moved and encouraged others to move according to it.

Through imagination ideas are formed, songs are composed and inventions are conceived. By imagination thoughts of "what if?" are pondered. Prophetic imagination inspires one to act or to dream. But unfortunately, if we fail to transform our thinking our imaginations remain in the fallen state in which they entered as a result of Adam's sin. Man's imagination was used for destructive, carnal lust and rebellion against God. Genesis 6:5 says, "God saw the wickedness of man was great in the earth, and that every imagination of the thoughts of his heart was only evil continually." Prophetic imagination has no boundaries. After the fall, man did not lose his ability to use imagination; however, the imagination became corrupted. Fortunately, through the power of the Holy Spirit we can cast down vain imaginations and redirect our thinking to bring forth God's purpose for our lives. In Genesis 11:6, the Lord acknowledges the ability of man to walk in greatness because of his ability to imagine. He said, "Behold the people is one and they have all one language and this they begin to do and now nothing will be restrained from them which they have imagined to do."

Jonas Clark in his article "Christian Living and Spiritual Growth: Unlocking Your Prophetic Imagination" states that "All creativity and innovation come through prophetic imagination." Everything that we now see, originated in the realm of the unseen. The God who knows our beginning and has seen our end has called us to greatness. Because of him, we can dream and dream big. He has high expectations of us and expects us to be fruitful, multiply, replenish, subdue and have dominion in the earth. We have the responsibility and the ability to transform our world. With Him, all things are possible.

We were designed with the facility to see the possibilities. Our transformed imaginations allows us to see what others cannot see. Everything exists because God saw it and caused it to come forth. As we are led by the Spirit of God, we are able to understand who we are and how we are made. Our design is made manifest. We are spirits with souls who dwell in bodies. Prior to salvation, we were separated from God because of sin. However, salvation has placed us in right standing with Him who created us. Because of this work, we see Him active in our lives and the possibilities are available to us.

Matthew 12:35 (KJV) states that, "*A good man out of the good treasure of the heart bringeth forth good things and an evil man out of the evil treasure bringeth forth evil things."* In its original form, the word treasure means *thesaurus* or *treasury*. The treasury is where truth is stored and is the dwelling place of prophetic imagination. It is where our dreams abide. It is the place where we *"bringeth forth good things."* What are you bringing forth? What are you imagining? What pictures are you painting? Consider your life, if you need to dream again, then dream again! In Christ, you have the wherewithal to achieve greatness. Get an expectation, imagine something new and set a purpose. If God be for us, who can be against us! Launch into the deep and engage your prophetic imagination. Write it down and make it plain so that you can run every time you read it!

Chapter 10

Transformational Thinking and Christian Scholarship

During the more than fifty years that I have been a part of the body of Christ, I have noticed that the impulse of modern and post-modern society is to compartmentalize our lives between things that are public and private, sacred and secular, work and play, and yes, even black and white. Modern and post-modern man, along with modern and post-modern society has lost his spiritual center, becoming fragmented and hurried – but only God knows for what! In this cultural milieu, the Christian scholar who bravely resists this impulse toward fragmentation finds the situation exacerbated due to two countervailing pressures that often pull in opposite directions. On one hand, the secular ethos of the university presses Christian scholars to conduct their research and teaching in purely secular terms and motifs. If Christian scholars want a place at the table, they must play by the rules of the academic game. A strict wall of separation between church and state exists, and any effort to tear down the wall is looked on with either suspicion or outright incredulity.

On the other hand, the Christian scholar is committed to a particular view of the world that is antithetical to the established secular ethos. The Christian universe is a God-centered universe. If Jesus is Lord, He is Lord of all areas of thought and life. In fact, the Bible claims that in Jesus *"are hidden all the treasures of wisdom and knowledge"* (Col. 2:3). Thus, the Christian scholar himself often becomes disintegrated, compartmentalizing his "scholarly life" from his "spiritual life" as he attempts to navigate between religious fundamentalism and accommodation-ism. Any attempts to invoke a Christian perspective to science (for example) in the university are quickly labeled as fundamentalist attempts to promote religion masquerading as science. Any attempts to utilize non-biblical conceptual schemes erected by thinkers such as Plato, Aristotle or Kant in order to shape and guide research and teaching are (sometimes) viewed by the church as selling out to accommodation-ism. The best result of these opposing pressures is that the Christian scholar is left in a sort of "no-man land" – viewed with suspicion by both the church and the university. Within the secular academy, religion is relegated to the sidelines. Religion is reserved for the scholar's personal life: meaningful to either the individual or one's own religious community only. This raises the question of whether or not there is a place in society for believers in Christ, who are transformational thinkers, and what scholars call "reality."

Transformational Thinking and Reality

Christianity, like secular institutions, has a claim about reality, a reality created and sustained by Christ. This simply alludes to the fact that the Christian worldview includes thoughts and mindsets about the way the world is. A transformational thinker, who is also a believer in Jesus Christ, has to have the ability to integrate his faith with his scholarship whenever he is involved in either explicit Christian activity or latent Christian word, such as research. This is an urgent matter in the twenty first century when we must have believers affecting every area of society and the marketplace. This is perhaps the place where the spiritual vocation or calling, becomes the occupation or work that brings glory to God, as worship flows from what we do.

Transformational thinkers can no longer afford to see the work of the Kingdom of God as being relegated to the local church, or various religions, denominations and reformations. We must be committed to pluralism so that the gospel message is proclaimed not as a system of values only, but as a truth that corresponds to reality. As such, the proclamation of the gospel becomes part of the continuing conversation that shapes both public policy and religious doctrine.

While reaching consensus on future plans to address current global challenges is far from easy, it seems that reductionist approaches that suggest a limited set of targeted interventions to improve these challenges, be they physical or mental health, economic, education, or whatever, around the world are inadequate. It seems that a comprehensive perspective should guide health practices, education, research, employment strategies and policy. The key is transformational thinking, tools and strategies that have the potential for transformational change in all the systems that affect lives globally. Three overarching themes span these tools and strategies: collaboration across disciplines, sectors and organizations; and transformational leadership. In a very limited way, let me define these strategies.

Collaboration across disciplines, sectors and organizations has to be listed first since the issues of society are too great to leave any sector out or uninvolved. Inter-professional collaboration is a key factor in initiatives designed to increase the effectiveness of care and services currently offered to the society. It is important that the concept of collaboration be well understood, because although the increasingly complex problems faced by professionals in every genre of life, are creating more interdependencies among them, we still have limited knowledge of the complexity of inter-professional relationships.

Transformational leadership is defined as a leadership approach that causes change in individuals and social systems. In its ideal form, it creates valuable and positive change in the followers with the end goal of developing followers into leaders. Enacted in its authentic form, transformational leadership enhances the motivation, morale and performance of followers through a variety of mechanisms. These include connecting the follower's sense of identity and self to the mission and the collective identity of the organization; being a role model for followers that inspires them; challenging followers to take greater ownership for their work, and understanding the strengths and weaknesses of followers, so the leader can align followers with tasks that optimize their performances.

No matter what the global issue may be, there is great reward in a synergistic approach to problem solving. There is an ancient proverb that alludes to the thought that we are better together and Deuteronomy 32:20 says, one can chase a thousand, but two can chase ten thousand. That is synergy. It is a must that we promote and involve ourselves in the multi- disciplinary efforts to solve the many atrocities of our world. The sacred needs the secular and the secular needs the sacred.

Holiness and Transformational Thinking

Even the simplest glance or gesture is open to misinterpretation when we *"see in a mirror, dimly"* (1 Cor. 13:12), while a blur as vast and dark as the "problem of evil" could daunt an intellect as impressive as Augustine's.

Perhaps all of us have experienced moments of introspection when we know as fully as we are known. These are moments when the mirror shatters and we come face to face with Truth. Sometimes it is frightening. The fleeting clarity of discovery reveals (as "in the twinkling of an eye") the fulfillment of the *"living hope"* the apostle Peter describes (1 Pet 1:3).

I doubt that the "scholarship of discovery" really ought to take priority over the other kinds of scholarship identified like integration, application, and teaching. I sense that most "discovery" is really "recovery. Yet, I appreciate the exhilaration of the "eureka" moment, and wish that it could be experienced much more regularly.

The word holiness was once seen as "detachment." Valued by early monks as a virtue, it has almost lost its positive connotation. Nowadays it is most often used in a negative sense, to mean the opposite of a healthy engagement with the world, and with other people. It conveys a sense of aloofness, a studied remoteness that signifies a lack of concern for others. The monastic interpretation of "detachment" and holiness could not be more different. In this tradition, it means not allowing either worldly values or self-centeredness to distract us from what is most essential in our relationship with God, and with each other.

Christian Scholarship and Transformational Thinking

A different way of thinking about the Christian vocation of scholarship is suggested by Jake Jacobsen and Rhonda Hustedt Jacobsen of Messiah College. In addition to encouraging Protestant scholars to draw on Christian denominational traditions in the book *Scholarship & Christian Faith: Enlarging the Conversation* , they ask what "traditions of spiritual practice" might mean for Christian scholarship? They conclude that:

"While the churchly theological traditions just described have been central for many Christian scholars, Christian faith transcends churchly affiliation and theological affinity. A person's faith is in some sense a gut-level reaction to the sacred.... When we speak of traditions of spirituality, what we have in mind is that holistic experience of the sacred—an experience of faith that involves the entire person: the combined physical, emotional, and intellectual dimensions of who we are as human beings...."

Piety or spirituality is almost always complex and multi-layered. Our personal response to God pulls us in different directions at the same time: wordless wonder, thankfulness, worship, prayer, joy, sorrow for the pain of the world, desire to serve others. For most of us, however, certain dimensions of spiritual practice ultimately become more important than others. Out of the many and varied impulses of piety, only some seem a natural fit; only some aspects of Christian practice demand our sustained attention.... Just because our divergent spiritualties push us in these different directions—just because we tend to spend more time and effort on one kind of spiritual activity rather than another—does not mean that we thereby dismiss other expressions of piety as inherently less valuable. It simply means that given the time constraints that define our lives, given the need to choose priorities, and given our own natural inclinations, we will find ourselves drawn to certain forms of piety or spirituality more than others. And those different spiritual dispositions can have an influence on the way we understand Christian scholarship. (pp. 90-91)[5]

They then consider how the six spiritual traditions described by Richard Foster (*Streams of Living Water, 2001*) could influence conceptions of Christian scholarship. I'll just touch on the two. First, the "*stream*" exemplified by Anthony of the Desert, Julian of Norwich, and Henri Nouwen:

The contemplative tradition of Christian piety emphasizes the mystical experience of God that comes through the life of prayer. It is a deeply personal form of spirituality and one that often draws individuals away from attachments to the world.... The contemplative tradition of spirituality has the goal of always living in the conscious presence of God. (91)[6]

Then, a bit less obvious, the second *tradition*:

The holiness tradition focuses on the development of Christian character through self-discipline and the cultivation of the virtues. The goal is the restructuring of the inner affections so that right living becomes a natural habit. (p. 91)

As examples of the "holiness" tradition, Foster mentions two seemingly different 16th century figures — Menno Simons and Ignatius Loyola, who "shared a sense of Christian faith as a way of life—a way of life that required the cultivation of certain dispositions like humility, a willingness to serve others, nonviolence, and introspective

---

[5] Jacobsen, Douglas, Jacobsen, R.H. (2004). Scholarship and Christian Faith: enlarging the conversation. New York, Oxford University Press

[6] Ibid, 91

self-criticism" — as well as Phoebe Palmer and Dietrich Bonhoeffer, in whose "lives we see a commitment to deny self and to conform fully to the requirements of the gospel, especially as expressed in Jesus' words in the Sermon on the Mount."(p.92)

Jacobsen and Jacobsen conclude:

The vocation of Christian scholarship is not necessarily central to any of these six traditions of spiritual practice, but each has implications that might apply to the academic life. The contemplative tradition reminds us of the need to make room for divine mystery in our academic interpretations of the world. The holiness tradition points to the fact that the habits we cultivate—either habits of virtue or habits of vice—have the potential to shape our scholarship in subtle ways for good or for ill. (p. 93)[7]

I am convinced that scholarship can serve to develop Christian character. I am sure that, as the Jacobsens suggest, our habits can shape our scholarship, but beyond whatever we discover (or recover) and how we interpret what we find, the very act of research is valuable for individual scholars and academic communities because it can cultivate "habits of virtue" like patience and humility — and, the virtue of joy.

---

[7] Ibid., 93

CHAPTER 11
HOLY INTELLIGENCE (HQ) AND THE BIBLE

If we are to ever optimize our pursuit of transformational thinking, there must be a discovering of Holy Intelligence. If we are to optimize our pursuit of Holy Intelligence and transformational thinking, there is no getting around the need to find the Source from which infinite and sovereign intelligence exists. From whom or from where does all knowledge exist? Is there only one Source, or are there many sources? Does the Source or sources share their intelligence? If so, with whom, and how is it acquired? Some of these questions I hope to answer in a future publication, as I research this serious matter.

I believe that it goes without saying that the truest definition of transformational thinking may simply be to think like the Source thinks. To those of us who believe in the God of creation, transformational thinking requires that my thinking aligns with the purpose, plan, promises, ways and ideas of the One, True and Holy God. This exposes us to Holy Intelligence: God's Intelligence.

The term Holy Intelligence (HQ) was given to me in prayer, upon noticing that this is an era that places great significance on intelligence.

There are major emphasis on Intelligence Quotient (IQ), Emotional Intelligence (EQ), Spiritual Intelligence (SQ), and Leadership Intelligence (LQ). However, I am convinced that there is little to no discussion on the ultimate, unchallengeable, unsearchable and all-knowing intelligence of all and that is the intelligence of God, which I refer to as Holy Intelligence (HQ). As a result, I am seeking to discover and recover what portions or quotients of God's Holy Intelligence can a believer possess, thus his HQ. Simply stated, each member of the Body of Christ possesses a portion or quotient of the vastness and limitlessness of God's sovereign knowledge, wisdom, understanding, power, and presence. That portion is the Believer's Holy Intelligence or HQ.

Holy Intelligence and the Bible

There is much written on spiritual intelligence, the philosophy that I will call the cousin of holy intelligence, but there is very little information on holy intelligence. This raises the question that must be answered, now or later: what is holy intelligence? Is it a concept that can only be embraced by those who believe in the One, True and Holy God? If so, to what extent can believers manifest or make known His love, wisdom, knowledge, power, and presence? Even for those who believe that they possess some measure of His divine nature (II Peter 1:3-4), how is it measured? I will refer to holy intelligence as the intelligence with which we translate into the earth the authentic love, presence, power, wisdom and knowledge of God to a world that He created and must be reacquainted with Him. It is the intelligence by which children of God convey the relationship between God and man, man to man, and man to God. It reflects the cross of Christ in its symbolism in that it points vertically to a Divine and human relationship, and horizontally to the man-to-man relationship. It is the intelligence by which believers live their lives in total harmony accordance to the purpose and plan of God. It begins by a divine revelation that gives an answer to questions like: "Who am I?' and "Why am I here?" It is simply tapping into the intelligence of the only One who is Holy, God, who is the creator of all things.

Just as in the case of spiritual intelligence, and perhaps more so, the Bible illustrates how this life pursuit leads to an eternal path of life and life more abundantly (John 10:10). Holy intelligence shifts the believers viewpoint from things that are temporal to things that are eternal *"what is seen is temporary, but what is unseen is eternal."* (2 Cor. 4:18). The ultimate direction to acquire and be sustained in this pathway that directs us to the eternal ways of God, cannot be found through research, or intellectual pursuit; it is provided through the exclusivity of the indwelling presence of God in the believer's spirit (John 14:17, I John 2:20) . The ultimate end of holy intelligence is realized when the believer empties himself of his own will and desires and takes on the divine nature of Christ (Phil. 2:5-8; II Peter 1:3-5). Holy intelligence comes by revelation through God's indwelling Spirit, who imparts spiritual truths into man's spirit, now made holy. It is the ability, through relationship with Jesus Christ, to access the holy mind, thoughts, wisdom, knowledge, and ways of God, the holy One. We will never access or comprehend the things of God without the illumination of the Holy Spirit. Paul declares, *"The man without the Spirit does not accept the things that come from the Spirit of God, for they are foolishness to him, and he cannot understand them, because they are spiritually discerned"* (1 Cor. 2:9-14; 2 Cor. 4:18). (Examine these scriptures for further reference -1 Cor. 2:10-14; John 14:16-17, 26; 15:26; 16:13-15; Eph. 1:17-19.)

Overview of Theories of Intelligence

Theories of intelligence fall into a three main types of models: *developmental* and *psychometric* models based on measurement concepts; and information processing models (Dillale, 2000)[8]

Development Model

There have been a number of approaches to the study of the development of intelligence. Some have sought to understand how intelligence develops in terms of changes in the factors of intelligence over time and changes in the amounts of the various abilities that children have. Many psychologists believe that intellectual development does not exhibit the kind of smooth continuity that the concept of mental age appears to imply. Rather, development seems to come in intermittent bursts, whose timing can differ from one child to another.

Psychometric Model

Psychometrics is a field of study concerned with the theory and technique of psychological measurement. One part of the field is concerned with the objective measurement of skills and knowledge, abilities, attitudes, personality traits, and educational achievement. Some psychometric researchers have concerned themselves with the construction and validation of assessment instruments such as questionnaires, tests, raters' judgments, and personality tests.

---

[8] http://www.researchgate.net/profile/Lisabeth_Dilalla/publication/234691150_Development_of_Intelligence_Current_Research_and_Theories/links/02e7e52d44cdc649c2000000.pdf

Informational Model

R.V.L. Hartley expanded on ideas about *information*. Publishing in the *Bell System Technical Journal*, Hartley developed the concept of information based on "physical as contrasted with psychological considerations."

In the first section of Hartley's paper, titled *The Measurement of Information* (1928), he noted that "information is a very elastic term." In fact, Hartley never adequately defines this core concept. Instead, he addresses the "precision of ... information" and the "amount of information." Information exists in the transmission of symbols, with symbols having "certain meanings to the parties communicating." When someone receives information, each received symbol allows the recipient to "eliminate possibilities," excluding other possible symbols and their associated meanings. "The precision of information depends upon what other symbol sequences might have been chosen;" the measure of these other sequences provides an indication of the amount of information transmitted.

In Howard Gardener's multiple intelligences (1983) he theorizes that these are "relatively autonomous human intellectual competences"[9] and that they are formed, adapted and expressed by individuals and cultures. They are independent, but they typically work in harmony. This is consistent with Charles Spearman's (1904) theory that intelligence is based on one common intellectual factor known as "g" for general intelligence. While Spearman recognized specific abilities or "s," each

---

[9] Gardner, Howard, (1993). Creating minds: an anatomy of creativity seen through the lives of Freud, Einstein, etc.. New York: Basic Books

requires a certain amount of g factor.[10] Please forgive my naiveté, but perhaps the "g" represents "God" and the "s" refers to the Holy "Spirit."

The Acquisition of Intelligence

The processes and core operations, by which knowledge is acquired, however, are more culture-general because they are based in human neurology and human cognitive capacity. For linguistic intelligence, these core operations include semantics, phonology, syntax, and pragmatics. For musical intelligence the principal constituent elements are pitch, rhythm, and timbre (pp. 104-105)[11], with which neurology and emotions have a critical modifying role. Gardner describes the core operations and developmental trajectory for the other "intelligences;" such as logical-mathematical, spatial, bodily-kinesthetic, and personal (inner- and interpersonal "intelligence"). Gardner freely concedes that there may be more or fewer "intelligences" than he describes even spiritual intelligence.[12] Emotional intelligence has received a fair amount of interest since 1985 when Wayne Payne wrote a dissertation on the topic. Mayer and Salovey (1993, 1995) and Mayer and Geher (1996) made other significant contributions to an understanding of emotional intelligence. They describe it as social intelligence that involves the ability to monitor one's own and others' emotions, to discriminate among various emotions, and to use the information to guide thought

---

[10] Spearman, Charles, (1904). General Intelligence. http://psychology.about.com/od/gindex/g/general-intelligence.htm

[11] Ibid, Gardner, pp. 104-105

[12] Gardner, ibid, pp. 104-105.

and action. According to Salovey and Mayer (1990)[13], it subsumes Gardner's inter- and intrapersonal intelligences. Daniel Goleman popularized the concepts and applied it to business success with his 1995 book "Emotional Intelligence."

For each type of intelligence that Gardner describes, he also describes different core operations that are involved in coming to know in any given domain. Each subject (e.g., music, math, or politics) differs in the core operations that relate those disciplines to the student. In all, perception of the otherness is partly based in neurology (e.g., visual or aural acuity and sensitivity to pitch relations), part information processing and pattern recognition (grammar, rhythm), and part nurture (educational intervention). How to know and manipulate the symbols and symbolic maps of any domain varies.

Robert and Michele Root-Bernstein (1999) take the theory of multiple intelligences a step further. They argue that "multiple intelligences" is not intelligence per se. Rather, they are the media through which intelligence is expressed. The artifacts created through these media are symptoms of intelligence. According to them, thinking and creativity precede logical and verbal expression, and is experienced by the individual in pre-verbal ways. Thus, "knowing something" is first experienced through the emotions, intuitions, visual images, and bodily feelings.[14] For example, one may hunt for just the right word by checking a thesaurus or dictionary. The right word, though, may be elusive and the individual proceeds with the best approximation

---

[13] Mayer, J.D. & Salovey, P. (1995). Emotional Intelligence and the construction and regulation of feelings. Applied and Preventive Psychology, 4, 197-208

[14] Rooty-Bernstein, R. and Root-Bernstein, M. (1999) Sparks of genius. Boston: Houghton Mifflin

that comes to mind. Later, when that right word pops up it is happily incorporated into its place.

There is a sense of relief in finding the right word that one already knew at an emotional or subconscious level. One who is high in verbal intelligence is more adept at naming emotions and readily finding the right word, while others struggle to express themselves. Paul lends support for this type of pre-verbal, visceral, or physical knowledge that is known before it can be expressed in words, if ever. He says we *"groan inwardly as we wait eagerly for our adoption as sons, the redemption of our bodies"* (Rom. 8:22-24) and *"if I pray in a tongue, my spirit prays, but my mind is unfruitful"* (1 Cor. 14:13-15).

Man's Pursuit for Intelligence

The Bible indicates that humans are created with a longing for eternity, a restlessness that reaches for but cannot fully know God and his ways (Eccl. 3:11). The individual must "translate" this pre-verbal, ill-defined knowledge into one or more of the different intelligences such as words, quantitative formulae, paintings, or music. Some things can be expressed in more than one way. An abstraction such as "love" can be expressed verbally, graphically or interpersonally.

Intelligence of any kind generally increases with age and maturation. Luke observed that the young Jesus grew physically and *"became strong in spirit"* (Luke 1:80). John Fowler (1995) has described stages in faith development in a manner similar to Jean Piaget's (1973) developmental approach to describing intelligence. Core operations in Piaget's model of cognitive development are the dual processes of assimilation and accommodation. In his classic work, Stages of faith: the psychology of human development (1995), Fowler describes a six-stage model of development from childhood to maturity. Because Fowler's model of stages of faith development is a developmental one, it will be of greatest interest to those who work with children. [15]

Holy Intelligence and Core Operations

Like spiritual intelligence, holy intelligence has as a fundamental core operation which is the ability to discern the phenomenon unique to a specific intelligence (whether color, musical sounds, spatial shapes, quantifiable objects, words, or physical, nonverbal cues). Spiritual matters are noted to be spiritually discerned, but unclear to others (1 Cor. 2:14). As Lisa Beardsley (2004) notes in her research, those who lack discernment become increasingly self-serving until society itself is corrupted and decays (Gen. 6:10-14; Jonah 1:2; 4:11; Rom. 1:21, 28-32).[16]

Who has discernment? In Psalm 19:12, the question is raised: "*Who can discern his errors?* Solomon was wise enough to ask God for discernment. (1 Kings 3:9; 12). Knowledge is elusive without discernment (Pr. 14:6). Therefore it is paramount that we seek after it. We must study and ponder the Word and pray. Our choices and our behavior are a reflection of our ability to discern. Discernment allows us to learn from our mistakes and excel in the things of God ("*rebuke a discerning man and he will gain knowledge,*" Pr. 19:25).

---

[15] Fowler, J.W. (1995). Stages of faith: the psychology of human development. San Francisco:Harper

[16] http://fae.adventist.org/essays/31Bcc_001-042.htm

Intellect in Scripture

In exploring how intelligence in Scripture is developed, Beardsley suggests that, "Creativity depends on prior knowledge that must be learned before it can be changed." Most people need at least 10 years to master a skill. Jesus exhibited his holy intelligence at the age of 12 in the temple and the people were amazed at his mastery. Matthew records that they were puzzled when he began to teach the people in the synagogue (Matthew 13:54-56). They knew that he was the son of a carpenter and that ordinary men were his brothers so how could he have such knowledge.

If one has holy intelligence, he/she can apply the principles to every area of life and be able to respond as Jesus would to any challenge that may arise-even ethical issues. Scriptures do not present to us what is "spiritual," but what is "holy." The intelligence we seek to develop in our lives, must not just bring us into a path that leads to spirituality, but to becoming a partaker of His holiness. This is by far a greater experience.

The Context of Relationships

Much learning happens in the context of relationships with other people and prayer is a means of communication and relationship with God. Prayer is also an attitude of openness and receptivity to spiritual issues. What can be known about God can also be shared and validated in the community of faith. Even God, who has the power to do so, does not use authority to command trust. Trust in God grows out of a relationship with him. Good teachers provide students with a relational epistemology (knowledge). This epistemology uses core operations so that the unknown (Truth, God) is perceived, evaluated, and interpreted. Core operations are the means by which a relationship is formed with the subject.

This is validated in community, and substantiated by evidence. Relationship thus becomes both a vehicle to and a context for knowledge. But solitude has a role as well. There is value in periods of silence. God's greatness is in stillness (Ps. 46:9-11) and our own purpose in life is found in response to his gently whispered, "What are you doing here?" (1 Kings 19:12-13). "In all creation," said Meister Eckhart (1260-1327), "there is nothing so like God as stillness."

Faith, Hope, Charity and Holy Intelligence

One of the indisputable manifestations of a believer's love for God, his Creator, is the love that he has for others. This is the greatest virtue among the three listed in I Corinthians 13:13, *"And now abideth faith, hope, charity, these three; but the greatest of these is charity* (love)." (*Emphasis is mine*)

Hebrews 11:1 is clear that faith is *"being sure of what we hope for and certain of what we do not see"*. Jesus is the *author and finisher of our faith*, on whom every believer is to focus his eyes on (Hebrews 12:2).

Hope, which is an assurance that God is who he claims to be, brings the believer to a place of rest (Acts 2:26; 26:6). This a feeling of expectation and desire that creates for each believer a life of aspiration, desire, ambition, trust and determination, in our daily lives. Romans 8:24 says, *"For we are saved by hope..."* It is clear in the study of the Bible that faith and hope are interrelated (Col. 1:5, 23), and can be affected by life experiences of others as we read and learn of them through the Word (Romans 15:4).

Faith is great, hope is great, but love is greatest. The common thread that knits and knots the fabric of truth in the Bible is the consistency and solidity of God's love. That love is the imputed love that directs the life of every believer who will yield to its power and demonstration. This power and demonstration makes the believer's God known (John 13:35).

Failure

The Bible does not present individuals who are born perfect and without sin, except for One, that being Christ. Instead, what we find are a number of examples that encourage and demonstrate that faults and failures are great experiences from which holy intelligence can grow and develop. Both the old and new testaments reflect that names changes were often reflections of spiritual encounters (Abram to Abraham, Jacob to Israel, Simon to Cephas, Saul to Paul, Sarai to Sarah). These encounters were life changing experiences and are reflective in the language of the believer when we speak of repentance. Repentance means to have a change of heart, a change of way and a turning from one's sins. Included in this process is a metamorphosis -a change in form. It is a turning away from the old *and* a rebirth *(anakainosis)*, a renewal, renovation and complete change for the better.

Chapter 12

Transformation as the Center of New Testament Theology

Research has sought to define the church in terms of metaphors and illustrations. Something as mysterious and transcendent as the church is hard to get our arms around and define. Allow me to suggest that the work and the presence of the local church is constantly "morphing." Too often we have static views of the nature and essence of the church and wonder why we get frustrated when things keep changing. But I want to make a case for the amorphous nature of the body of Christ. The process of change and transformation is more fundamental to the nature of the church than its polity, tradition of worship practices, etc.

This is emphasized by Paul's choice of language in his letters. It is highlighted in the New Testament by the morph root words he uses. Look at the passages below:

Philippians 2:6-7   Jesus originally was in the form (*morph*) of God but humbled himself to the form (*morph*) of a servant.

Galatians 4:19	Paul expresses his personal agony and inner angst like that of the pains of childbirth, until Christ is formed (*morph*) in his readers.
Romans 12:2	Paul admonishes his readers not to live conformed to the pattern of this world, rather they are to be transformed (*morph*) by the renewing of their minds.
2 Corinthians 3:8	Turning to the Lord, lifts the veil of the heart so that believers can reflect the Lord's glory. In this process Paul's readers are being transformed (*morph*) into the likeness of Jesus with ever-increasing glory.

As the Scripture shows, Paul envisioned spiritual formation, transformation and renewal to be at the heart of community life in Christ. Rigid concepts about how people ought to behave and how programs ought to function, and how budgets ought to be spent, all run counter to this notion. Instead of seeing the church as a business to run, people to manipulate and programs to put on, we need to be counter-cultural in our perspective of the local congregation. Since Jesus is the greatest example of "*morph-ing*" we have, it makes sense to think that his followers would be living examples of "*morph-ing*" also. But practically, what does this mean for ministers, elders, deacons, teachers, ministry leaders, and members of the local church?

Allow me to suggest the following:

- Servant-hood takes on a diversity of shapes
- We do not allow the world to squeeze us into its mold
- As faithful Christians, we change from the inside out: heart and mind
- We are daily being changed into the likeness of Jesus

No wonder the local church seems to be constantly changing! It is inherent in the DNA of congregational life. Lives are constantly changing because of circumstances. But on a deeper level, we are changing because we are in the process of being "*morph-ed*" daily. This prepares us for the amorphous nature of relationships, problems, life situations, etc. This helps us take on more ownership of the changing of our brothers and sisters in Christ. This is why Paul could agonize like a woman in childbirth. Instead of pulling our hair out because the organizational, institutional aspect of church life is not happening, we trade that for agonizing over lack of change (*morph*) in the lives of our fellow believers.

God in Transformation

Only God can change the human heart and transform it by the working of his Spirit. The Spirit of God takes the raw material of clay and molds it into the image of Christ. This takes on a lovely diversity of appearance as each one is gifted differently. Ultimately, the inside "*morph-ing*" process will show itself on the outside. Changed hearts and minds slowly *morph* into the likeness of Jesus.

When we remember this, we are made free from two fears: the fear that things will change and the fear that they will not. Understanding "m*orphing*" helps us trust and praise the Lord for the results of his church, and for his work of transformation in our congregations!

There is a consistent idea that flows from all of Paul's letters: *Ministry is participation in God's work of transforming the community of faith until it is 'blameless' at the coming of Jesus".*[17] This working

---

[17] Thompson, James W. (2006), Pastoral ministry according to Paul: A biblical vision, p. 150, Grand Rapids, MI, Baker Academics

definition of ministry is counter-cultural to most of the contemporary thinking regarding church life today. First, it recognizes that ministry is a response to God's work. Second, it rightly restores the place of community in the experience of faith. And, thirdly, it sees formation of Christian character from an eschatological viewpoint and not merely as an ethical goal. Out of this Pauline model, three things are highlighted:

- Community formation that is connected with the "messiness of church life"
- An awareness of living between the times
- Holiness of character that will be presented as "blameless" at the Parousia.

From this tripartite model of ministry, we see that Paul's ultimate aim is to present a cross-shaped believing community that grows away from selfishness and is able to respond to the needs of others. This transformation of self as a work of the "new creation" is seen by Paul to be a work of the Spirit within the body of Christ. This formation provides the concern of his pastoral care and vision.

This provides for us a theological and exegetical foundation for viewing contemporary ministry. This shows us the centrality of the "transformation" language (i.e. Paul's vocabulary that use the "*morph*" stem in Greek), in Paul's understanding of the nature of the new creation.

It is my perspective that the center of Pauline theology is NOT justification by faith; rather, it is a theology of transformation. Paul's pastoral vision of transformation focuses more on ecclesiology than on an individual's personal response to the gospel. Paul does not concede his ministry to the point of allowing people to live in their weakness and sins. Rather, he demands transformation into the likeness and image of the crucified and emptied Christ.

Transformed by the Power of God

Systematic theologians often include within the category of sanctification the whole process of transformation, growth and maturation in Christ that is God's promise to us in the New Testament. In popular speech, this is the process of becoming more and more holy. However, a careful examination of the New Testament use of the verb 'to sanctify" (*hagiazein*) shows that the focus is on the beginning of the Christian life rather than its progress. Sanctification or consecration is a way of describing how God takes hold of us through conversion and brings us into relationship with himself as the Holy One. As a consequence, we are called 'the holy ones' or 'the saints' (*hoi hagioi*). The challenge is to express that holiness in everyday obedience. But how do we make progress in the Christian life and grow to be more like the Lord Jesus Christ?

The Transforming Knowledge of God

There is extensive teaching about knowing the Lord in the Gospel and the First Letter of John. The link between knowing, believing and the work of the Holy Spirit is explored. In view of the claim that 'you have been anointed by the Holy One, and you all have knowledge' (1 Jn.2:20), the tests of a true relationship with God are discussed. In view of the claim that 'you have no need that anyone should teach you' (1 Jn. 2:27), the role of Christian teaching in promoting the true knowledge of God is examined.

New Covenant theology is central to New Testament thinking about the saving work of Christ and the way it is appropriated by believers. It has profound implications for Christian ministry, both with respect to evangelism and the nurture of believers. It is the basis of much teaching about perseverance, growth and change. It is a key for understanding the differences between pre-Christ and post-Christ experiences of God. In terms of the Bible's teaching as a whole, it shows how the Christian dispensation is a fulfilment and perfection of the covenant first established by God with Abraham and his offspring.

Chapter 13
Transformational Leadership

One of the hallmarks of Transformational Leadership is the connections or relationships formed between leaders and followers. Transformational Leaders are deeply committed to their followers. This model bears witness that relationship is stronger than legalism, or relationships that are bound together by rituals or organizational codes.

Transformational Leaders are interested in more than group performance. They are interested in seeing each person fulfill his/her potential. The Transformational Leader is interested in seeing positive change in his followers. Transformational Leaders generally see the group and the individual succeed far beyond their expectations.

Transformational Leadership starts with the development of a vision, a view of the future that will excite potential followers. Often this vision is developed in concert with the followers.

The Construct of Leadership

In Mark W. McCloskey's article entitled, *What is Transformational Leadership?*[18], he presents the following definition of leadership from the baseline of *construct*.

McCloskey states that "a construct is concept or organizing structure hypothesized to underlie an observable phenomenon." Leadership is a construct. It is the art and science of taking individuals and communities to a new and better place.

Managing and Leading Contrasted

The term "lead" is derived from an Old English term "*lithan*" and an Old French term "*leden*", meaning "to go", or "to cause to go with oneself"; and thus "to guide or show the way." The term connotes a sense of movement or journey from one place to another. Jesus used the word in this way, albeit in a negative sense. "Can a blind man *lead* a blind man? Will they not both fall into a pit?" (Luke 6:39).[19]

The word leadership is a noun, the term "lead" is a verb. Leaders lead others to unfamiliar places- new territory. They act as a guide by demonstrating to those who are following how it should be done. To lead is different than to manage. Manage means to grasp a thing in order to ensure that the desired end is accomplished. These are two different constructs. In managing, there is a discriminating use of things in order to achieve an expected end. Conversely, leadership involves the rallying of individuals

---

[18] http://people.bethel.edu/~pferris/otcommon/TransformationalLeadership.pdf
[19] http://people.bethel.edu/~pferris/otcommon/TransformationalLeadership.pdf

to complete a task that may or may not involve risks, but that are nevertheless worthwhile.

Management involves the manipulation of something that already exists. It affords one the opportunity to control the situation because it operates based on what is known and ascertainable. Leadership, on the other hand, demands that one has the ability to orchestrate a new situation. Leadership is squarely about the unknown and the unforeseen. It requires commitment, passion, determination, inspiration, courage, and integrity.

Defining and Describing Transformational Leadership

The term *Transformational leadership* is relatively recent, first coined in 1973 by J. V. Downton in his book, *Rebel Leadership: commitment and charisma in a revolutionary process*. According to leadership theorist James MacGregor Burns, transformational leadership is "A relationship of mutual stimulation and elevation that converts followers into leaders and convert leaders into moral agents."[20]

Francis Yammarino (1994, p.28) describes the process of transformational leadership as, "…the transformational leader arouses heightened awareness and interests in the group or organization, increases confidence, and moves followers gradually from concerns for existence to concerns for achievement and growth… in short, transformational leaders develop their followers to the point where followers are able to take on leadership roles and perform beyond established standards or goals…"[21]

---

[20] Burns, James MacGregor, (2003). Transforming Leadership. NY: Grove Press

[21] Bernard Bass and Bruce Avolio (ed.) *Improving Organizational Effectiveness Through Transformational Leadership, Sage Publications, Thousand Oaks, CA, 1994, p.28).*

According to Bernard Bass (1985), "Transformational leaders attempt and succeed in raising colleagues, subordinates, followers, clients or constituencies to a greater level of awareness about issues of consequences"

I believe that a great definition of transformational leadership is, the process of creating, sustaining and enhancing leader-follower, follower-leader, and leader-leader partnerships in pursuit of a common vision, in accordance with shared values and on behalf of the community in which leaders and followers jointly serve. In the context of this process of service and partnership, both the leader and follower, and eventually the entire community experience increasing levels of congruity with the ethos, vision and values of the community.

Transformational leaders initiate and sustain a process of partnership in and through which leaders and followers and the entire community experience increasing levels of congruity between the vision and values they espouse, and their character, capacities and conduct. Transformational leaders are catalysts for a process of change in which leaders, followers and the community become more and more like who they aspire to be and act more and more in accordance with what they want to do. Leaders invite followers and the entire community to journey with them to a better future, which more fully embodies their personal and collective vision and honors their shared values.

Faithful Stewardship

To be a transformational leader requires faithful stewardship. Transformational leaders must wisely use the resources that are made available to them. They have been provided to them to accomplish the task of effectively leading others. Leaders must never forget that they are servants. They occupy a low status for a great undertaking.

Transformational Servant Leadership

Robert K. Greenleaf first coined the phrase "servant leadership" in his 1970 essay, *"The Servant as a Leader."*[22] However, it's an approach that people have used for centuries.

The servant leader, is a "servant first" – the focus is on the needs of others, especially team members, before you consider your own. You acknowledge other people's perspectives, give them the support they need to meet their work and personal goals, involve them in decisions where appropriate, and build a sense of community within your team. This leads to higher engagement, more trust, and stronger relationships with team members and other stakeholders. It can also lead to increased innovation.

Servant leadership is not a leadership style or technique as such. Rather it's a way of behaving that you adopt over the longer term. However, servant leadership is problematic in hierarchical, autocratic cultures where managers and leaders are expected to make all the decisions. Here, servant leaders may struggle to earn respect.

How to Become a Servant Leader

According to Larry C. Spears, former president of the Robert K. Greenleaf Center for Servant Leadership, these are the 10 most important characteristics of servant leaders.[23][24] Once you've decided to prioritize

---

[22] https://greenleaf.org/products-page/the-servant-as-leader/

[23] Spears, Larry C. (2002). Focus on Leadership: servant leadership for the twenty first century. NY: John Wiley & Sons

[24] "Character and Servant Leadership: 10 Characteristics of Effective, Caring Leaders" by Larry C. Spears, published in "The Journal of Virtues and Leadership," Vol. 1, Issue 1.

other people's needs over your own in the long term, you can work on developing your skills in each area. Let's look at how you can do this.

1. *Listening* – You will serve people better when you make a deep commitment to listening intently to them and understanding what they are saying. To improve your listening skills, give people your full attention, take notice of their body language, avoid interrupting them before they have finished speaking, and give feedback on what they say.

2. *Empathy* - Servant leaders strive to understand other people's intentions and perspectives. You can be more empathetic by putting aside your viewpoint temporarily, valuing others' perspectives, and approaching situations with an open mind.

3. *Healing* - This characteristic relates to the emotional health and "wholeness" of people, and involves supporting them both physically and mentally. Make sure that your people have the knowledge, support and resources they need to do their jobs effectively, and that they have a healthy workplace. Then take steps to help them be happy and engaged in their roles.

4. *Self-Awareness* - Self-awareness is the ability to look at yourself, think deeply about your emotions and behavior, and consider how they affect the people around you and align with your values. You can become more self-aware by knowing your strengths and weaknesses, and asking for other people's feedback on them. Also, learn to manage your emotions, so that you consider how your actions and behavior might affect others.

5. *Persuasion* - Servant leaders use persuasion – rather than their authority – to encourage people to take action. They also aim to build

consensus in groups, so that everyone supports decisions. There are many tools and models that you can use to be more persuasive, without damaging relationships or taking advantage of others. You should build on your expert power. When people perceive you as an expert, they are more likely to listen to you when you want to persuade or inspire them.

6. *Conceptualization* - This characteristic relates to your ability to "dream great dreams," so that you look beyond day-to-day realities to the bigger picture. If you're a senior leader in your organization, work through and develop a robust organizational strategy. Then, whatever level you are on, create mission and vision statements for your team, and make it clear how people's roles tie in with your team's and organization's long-term objectives. Also, develop long-term focus so that you stay motivated to achieve your more distant goals, without getting distracted.

7. *Foresight* - Foresight is when you can predict what is likely to happen in the future by learning from past experiences, identifying what is happening now, and understanding the consequences of your decisions. Also, learn to trust your intuition – if your instinct is telling you that something is wrong, listen to it!

8. *Stewardship* - Stewardship is about taking responsibility for the actions and performance of your team, and being accountable for the role team members play in your organization. Take time to think about your own values, as well as those of your organization, so that you know what you will and will not stand for. Lead by demonstrating the values and behaviors that you want to see in others, and have the

confidence to stand up to people when they act in a way that is not aligned with those values and behaviors.

9. *Commitment to the Growth of People* - Servant leaders are committed to the personal and professional development of everyone on their teams. To develop your people, make sure that you use assessment tools to understand their developmental needs and give them the skills they need to do their jobs effectively. Find out what their personal goals are, and see if you can give them projects or additional responsibilities that will help them achieve these.

10. *Building Community* - Building a sense of community within your organization. You can do this by providing opportunities for people to interact with one another across the organization. Design your workspace to encourage people to chat informally away from their desks, and dedicate the first few minutes of meetings to non-work-related conversations. Encourage people to take responsibility for their work, and remind them how what they do contributes to the success and overall objectives of the organization.

CHAPTER 14

TRANSFORMATIONAL THINKING IS HEALTHY THINKING

Could it be that unhealthy living is birthed out of unhealthy thinking? Let me identify ten patterns of healthy thinking, core habits of the mind that come from an inward divine life and lead to fruitful outward action.

In one of the prior chapters, I introduced transformational thinking from the perspective of looking at God. The continuous experience of inward union with Christ is the source and center of all other healthy thinking behaviors. This is an inward choice to look at Him, by His Spirit. *And we all, with unveiled face, beholding the glory of the Lord, are being transformed into the same image from one degree of glory to another. For this comes from the Lord who is the Sprit (2 Cor. 3:18 ESV).*

The understanding of our oneness with Christ is the key that unlocks the door to transformational thinking. Jesus prayed for this union and understanding as He prayed before His crucifixion (John 17:20-23). I am so emphatic about this to the extent that I believe that believers in Christ Jesus have the wherewithal to live the best lives of any other people in the world. As our relationship with God excels, so ought our manifestations of the Christ life. *Beloved, I wish above all things that thou mayest prosper and be in health, even as ty soul prospereth (3 John 2).*

...If a man abides in me and I in him, he will bear much fruit; apart from me you can do nothing (John 15:5).

Through our oneness with Christ, each believer is capable of living out of Christ's inward life, supernatural manifestations of His victory, power, presence, and love. Those who live this way quickly discover that they desire nothing more than to please Him. As their thinking is transformed, they strive to optimize the fullness of His glory that can flow through them. This is the abundant life.

Paul, the Apostle writes, *And we pray this in order that you may live a life worthy of the Lord and may please Him in every way: bearing fruit in every good work, growing in the knowledge of God, being strengthened with all power according to His glorious might so that you may have great endurance and patience, and joyfully giving thanks to the Father...(Col. 1:10-12).*

Leadership Letters presents the idea of healthy leadership in the most profound Biblical way that I have ever read; let me share it with you.

"This is an inward growth orientation, a decision to move forward, a choice to act with purpose expecting growth, ultimate victory and fruitfulness. This comes directly from looking at God. *...If God is for us, who can be against us? (Rom. 8:31)* God created the universe – there is nothing too hard for Him! *Ah, Sovereign LORD, you have made the heavens and the earth by your great power and outstretched arm. Nothing is too hard for you (Jer. 32:17).*

Running Over

Transformational leaders look for and expect more. They are never satisfied with the notion of the cup being half full. They are looking for a cup that is running over. They are resolute that by the power and grace of the only true and living God that there will be growth and that those who they are leading will overcome! Failure is only temporary. Lessons will be learned and life shall spring forth! *If we are thrown into the blazing furnace, the God we serve is able to save us from it, and He will rescue us from your hand, O king. But even if He does not, we want you to know, O king, that we will not serve your gods or worship the image of gold you have set up (Dan. 3:17-18). ....Christ will be exalted in my body, whether by life or by death (Phil. 1:20).*

Confidence!

Caleb said, *Now give me this hill country that the LORD promised me that day. You yourself heard then that the Anakites were there and their cities were large and fortified, but, the LORD helping me, I will drive them out just as He said (Josh 14:12).* Transformational thinkers exude confidence. This is transformational thinking at its best! Transformational thinkers believe God regardless of the circumstances that they face. *We should go up and take possession of the land, for we can certainly do it (Num 13:30).*

Because Caleb followed the Lord without wavering, he had the promise that he would see the promised land. *[Caleb] will see [the land], and I will give him and his descendants the land he set his feet on, because he followed the LORD wholeheartedly (Deut 1:36; cf. Num. 32:12 AMP).*

Transformational thinkers *act* with confidence and boldness. They demand victory and work towards that end. They not only know that God is for them, but they act on that truth. Defeat is not an option.

Divine Vision

Our inward life with Christ is played out in our outward effectiveness as leaders. Transformational leaders must put God first. They must look to Him for everything and expect Him to do what He has declared in His word that He will do. Transformational leaders are infused with divine vision. Therefore, they see what He sees. Their relationship with Him, causes them to even think as He thinks. God's inward and active presence in their lives is all about the fulfillment of His purpose. They serve a living God and their relationship with Him provokes them to move forward believing and determined to be involved in the manifestation of His will. They have no doubt in His ability to fulfill His promise!

Potential! That's what healthy leader sees-potential. God allows them to see it everywhere they look. They see the gifts, talents and callings of family members, friends, coworkers and fellow-worshippers. Even in the darkest situations they see great potential. No situation is hopeless. There is victory on every side!

Jesus and Paul, Our Examples

Jesus was a prime example of this orientation to growth. He had a passion for the highest. When He looked at The Twelve, he did not see men who would simply catch fish and perform other duties as assigned, he saw world changers. He saw men with the potential to transform nations. *And this gospel of the kingdom will be preached in the whole world as a testimony to all nations... Therefore go and make disciples of all nations... (Matt. 24:14; 28:19).*

Like Jesus, Paul did not see the church of his day in its current state, he saw the Bride of Christ without spot or wrinkle or any such thing! *...Christ loved the church and gave Himself up for her to make her holy, cleansing her by the washing with water through the word, and to present her to Himself as a radiant church, without stain or wrinkle or any other blemish, but holy and blameless (Eph. 5:25-27; cf. 3:16-19; 4:12-16; John 17:21-22).*

Healthy leaders believe God for His best. They thrive in crisis and look for opportunities to transform organizations and ministries that are on the brink of failure. They are always looking for new ventures and adventures. Mobilization is what they do. They can take a scattered team and make it successful. They are not content until they have given their all and have provoked others to do the same. They are risk takers. They lead! They are not afraid to go first. They plunge into new, sometimes dangerous, and always unpredictable territory. They take us to places we've never been before, and probably could never find on our own. Their faith compels us. Their vision compels us and constrains us to fully engage and move forward. *Not that I have already obtained all this, or have already been made perfect, but I press on to take hold of that for which Christ Jesus took hold of me. Brothers, I do not consider myself yet to have taken hold of it. But one thing I do: Forgetting what is behind and straining toward what is ahead, I press on toward the goal to win the prize for which God has called me heavenward in Christ Jesus (Phil. 3:12-14).*

Chapter 15

Rules of Engagement: Connecting the Dots

Now, let's take a look at how transformational leadership works. Transformational leadership theory makes the following assumptions about how the process of leader-follower engagement works. We might call these the rules of engagement, or connecting the dots.

The Basis

Transformational leadership is based on core values that are attached to extraordinary vision. Long-lasting and transformative change occurs when followers who have great potential are connected to extraordinary vision and core values. Change occurs in the leaders, the followers and in the lives of those who may be recipients or participants of any actions taken. In this atmosphere, a culture is formed that can ensure a continued constructive exchange between leaders and followers and sustainable growth within any organization.

Anyone who desires to engage in transformational leading must be in the process of transformation. None of us ever "arrive." We are ever learning and coming into the knowledge of the truth. Our goal should be to always embrace this process and be willing to take others along on our journey of development. To this end, a transformational leader must be a transformational partner. As a partner, he fully engages his followers in the process of transformation which reflects the vision and values that he embraces.

Measurable Outcomes

Goals are achieved because of the commitment of leaders and followers to engage in the process of transformation. Not only do leaders and followers benefit, but also communities. Even though outcomes are often unpredictable and uncontrollable, a pattern of "beyond expectation" outcomes is initiated.

Chain Reaction

A chain reaction occurs among individual followers, leaders and the broader community. The vision and values of the community become paramount. They take precedence over the personal agendas and task oriented actions of the leaders and followers. Leaders and followers must engage in a covenant commitment to focus on what is most important-- the higher order outcomes of the community. The focus cannot merely be on the task at hand, but the long-term goal must be in view.

An Ongoing Community Process

Transformational leaders and followers are social architects and catalysts for remarkable change. They help to design, sustain and grow healthy transformational communities. This takes an unwavering commitment to the vision and values of the community. Leaders must never allow their expectations to wane, but remain confident in the ability of the team to bring about transformational change. Followers must become transformational leaders and transformational leaders must become synergists in bringing about continuous change that is a reflection of the hearts and habits of the community. A healthy transformational community is inevitable in this environment. It may not be perfect, but it is growing and has the capacity to expand its sphere of influence as its vision prescribes.

Connected Beyond The Event

In transactional leadership, the leader and followers engage in a task, but after its completion, go their separate ways. There is no long term connection made. James MacGregor Burns (2003) writes, "The object in these cases is not a joint effort for persons with common aims acting for the collective interests of followers, but a bargain to aid the individual interests of persons or groups going their separate ways" (p.425). The event may have been successful, but it failed to produce a partnership among the participants. Transformational leadership, however, is very different. Leaders and followers stay connected beyond the event. They allow themselves to become a part of a community beyond their individual needs and agendas. They connect to the vision and the core values of the community.

A Legacy of Transformation

Transformational leaders look beyond the moment and see the future. They invest in preparing future community leaders. The vision speaks to longevity and sustainability. It cannot cease with the demise of the leader. It is necessary for each generation of transformational leaders to prepare the next generation of transformational servants. Transformational leaders must commit to leaving a legacy.

In *transactional theory*, because there is no partnership and no commitment to building a legacy, followers remain followers. They may be great followers, but they are not given the opportunity to go beyond that realm. Transactional leaders do not develop skills that are beneficial to him or to those that follow and the followers are stagnated by this failure.

However, in *transformational theory*, not only are tasks accomplished, but the followers are better equipped to one day become effective transformational leaders themselves. In the exchange between leaders and followers, leaders provoke followers to go deeper and to reach higher. The results are life-changing. When leaders and followers engage in this way, each ascends beyond their current positions and not only is growth seen in their lives, but also in the lives of those connected to them- the larger community. From their new posture, they are able to identify new needs and opportunities for service. Their capacities have been enlarged to take on new territory. Emerging from this experience are a new generation of transformational leaders who have the ability to continue to breathe life into the vision.

CHAPTER 16

CHOOSING THE RIGHT EMERGING TRANSFORMATIONAL LEADERS

While it is important for transformational leaders to ensure that they are grooming followers to ultimately become leaders, they can only successfully prepare a few at a time. To be effective the transformational leader must commit himself/herself wholly to the task. First, he must pray about whom to choose. Unfortunately, too often we spend more time trying to train people than we do in identifying the right people. Unfortunately, for most people, formal development programs are not enough to prepare them to be effective leaders.

As Jesus walked beside the Sea of Galilee, he saw Simon and his brother Andrew casting a net into the lake, for they were fishermen. "Come, follow me," Jesus said, "and I will make you fishers of men." At once they left their nets and followed him. When he had gone a little farther, he saw James son of Zebedee and his brother John in a boat, preparing their nets. Without delay he called them, and they left their father Zebedee in the boat with the hired men and followed him (Mark 1:16-20).

He came to Derbe and then to Lystra, where a disciple named Timothy lived, whose mother was a Jewess and a believer, but whose father was a Greek. The brothers at Lystra and Iconium spoke well of him. Paul wanted to take him along on the journey... (Acts 16:1-3).

This process is about more than academic ability; it is about having the spirit of a leader. So the transformational leader has to be willing to take his time in the identification process. Listed below are a few steps that you can follow when seeking to identify emerging transformational leaders:

1. Consider those who others would deem unlikely- take a risk.

   Jesus chose fisherman who were uneducated and limited in their experiences, yet they trusted the Lord and followed Him (John 1:46; Matt. 14:26; 20:21, 24; Luke 9:49, 52-54; Acts 4:13). Jesus believed in their potential. He saw greatness in them and committed Himself to pull it out of them. Jesus did not care about the opinions of others, he chose Matthew who everyone hated and Simon who was fickle! He was willing to take the risk because he looked beyond the natural and saw who they really were. He knew they had the inward characteristics to become transformational leaders. He needed men with passion to do what he was calling them to do.

2. Be patient and pray before making a choice.

   If Jesus needed to pray before He chose the Twelve, it would behoove us to do the same when we are selecting leaders. *One of those days Jesus went out to a mountainside to pray, and spent the night praying to God. When morning came, he called his disciples to him and chose twelve of them, whom he also designated apostles... (Luke 6:12-13).* Paul admonishes Timothy not to be hasty in the laying on of hands (i.e., in choosing and appointing new leaders)... *(1 Tim. 5:22).* The multitudes followed Jesus, but He only selected a few to be His disciples who ultimately became great leaders within the church. We cannot select people for leadership because we think it is a good idea, to fill quotas or to make friends.

3. Consider the fruit of those they have followed previously.

This may tell you something about the leadership qualities they have learned and/or acquired. The past can be a good predictor of the future. *The brothers at Lystra and Iconium spoke well of him (i.e. Timothy). Paul wanted to take him along on the journey, so he circumcised him because of the Jews who lived in that area, for they all knew that his father was a Greek (Acts 16:2-3).*

4. Get Recommendations

The brothers at Lystra and Iconium spoke well of him. Paul wanted to take him along on the journey... (Acts 16:2-3; cf. 6:3; 1 Tim. 3:7)

Others may know your potential mentees better than you. Listen! Others can be a wealth of information that could make a tremendous difference in identifying ones true character. Peer input should be valued. Often leaders are selected based on limited information. We fail to do our due diligence as leaders and often suffer the consequences of our choices- putting the life of our organizations at risk and subjecting followers to the damaging effects of poor leadership.

5. Look for the emerging leader to have a relationship with Christ

    The emerging leader must have a genuine relationship with Jesus Christ. This relationship will be the source of his character as well as his endurance during hard times. In addition, he will not compromise his integrity for the sake of being accepted by man. Being accepted by the Maker of heaven and earth will be sufficient!

6. Look for a Servant's Heart

    Emerging leaders must have a servant's heart. They must be willing to suffer for the sake of the ministry and be totally committed to it.

    Paul wanted to take him along on the journey, so he circumcised him because of the Jews who lived in that area, for they all knew that his father was a Greek (Acts 16:3). The kingdom of heaven is like treasure hidden in a field.

When a man found it, he hid it again, and then in his joy went and sold all he had and bought that field. Again, the kingdom of heaven is like a merchant looking for fine pearls. When he found one of great value, he went away and sold everything he had and bought it (Mat. 13:44-45).

It is difficult for followers to follow a leader who is not willing to make necessary sacrifices. Leadership is not about fame and fortune. It is not about gathering more titles to put in front of your name. It is a privilege to serve and that should be the leader's focus. When Jesus' disciples sought the highest places in His kingdom, He taught them a profound lesson: *They replied, "Let one of us sit at your right and the other at your left in your glory."... Jesus called them together and said, "You know that those who are regarded as rulers of the Gentiles lord it over them, and their high officials exercise authority over them. Not so with you. Instead, whoever wants to become great among you must be your servant, and whoever wants to be first must be slave of all. For even the Son of Man did not come to be served, but to serve, and to give his life as a ransom for many (Mark 10:37. 42-45).*

The Christian leader must realize that even in serving, he is only doing his duty.

Suppose one of you had a servant plowing or looking after the sheep. Would he say to the servant when he comes in from the field, "Come along now and sit down to eat"? Would he not rather say, "Prepare my supper, get yourself ready and wait on me while I eat and drink; after that you may eat and drink"? Would he thank the servant because he did what he was told to do? So you also, when you have done everything you were told to do, should say, "We are unworthy servants; we have only done our duty" (Luke 17:7-10).

Leadership is a costly endeavor. One must be willing to embrace the cost!

7. Look for genuine love.

Jesus requires that we express our love for Him in our love and commitment to His people.

The third time he said to him, "Simon son of John, do you love me?" Peter was hurt because Jesus asked him the third time, "Do you love me?" He said, "Lord, you know all things; you know that I love you." Jesus said, "Feed my sheep (John 21:17).

We love because he first loved us. If anyone says, "I love God," yet hates his brother, he is a liar. For anyone who does not love his brother, whom he has seen, cannot love God, whom he has not seen. And he has given us this command: Whoever loves God must also love his brother (1 John 4:19-21).

Leaders are not called to misuse or abuse the people of God. They are not a part of an organization, church or any other entity to promote the personal agenda of the leader. Leaders must love the people of God from a pure heart. *I have no one else like him, who takes a genuine interest in your welfare. For everyone looks out for his own interests, not those of Jesus Christ (Phil. 2:20-21).*

8. Look for responsibility and accountability

Emerging leaders should already have vision. They should be ready to take the lead and should have a track record of completing assignments despite constraints.

Emerging transformational leaders should have a teachable spirit and should be accountable. They must be open to instruction and correction. They should always be looking for opportunities to learn (Matt 25:14 -30).

9. Look for those who think-big and "outside the box."

Avoid people with singular or narrow vision. Most tasks will require a multi-disciplinary approach guided by a leader who has the ability to think across departmental or organizational issues. This ability is what distinguishes a leader from a manager. A manager tends to have singular focus. His concern is his area and that alone. Big thinkers understand that it is not just about their area, but about other areas as well, as each are interconnected. As a result, big thinkers have a better understanding of how to use resources and finances to meet needs. Their vision is for the organization, not just their area within the organization. This type of leader not only thinks big, but also outside of the box. They are always asking the Lord to make them more effective and efficient in their assignments. They are always looking for ways to make the greatest impact. This requires that the emerging transformational leader be constructive in his/her assessments of a situation not critical. Constructive criticism is followed by solutions or suggestions that are appropriate to the situation. However, in thinking outside of the box, the leader must still be practical. Time and resources are precious and cannot be wasted on impracticalities.

10. Look for a desire to help others succeed.

Emerging transformational leaders should not be consumed with their own success, but they be invested in helping others succeed.

Do nothing out of selfish ambition or vain conceit, but in humility consider others better than yourselves. Each of you should look not only to your own interests, but also to the interests of others (Phil. 2:3-4).

11. Look for one who thinks highly, but not more highly.

For by the grace given me I say to every one of you: Do not think of yourself more highly than you ought, but rather think of yourself with sober judgment, in accordance with the measure of faith God has given you (Rom. 12:3).

Those who demand perfection from themselves and others will not make good leaders. Effective leaders must recognize that everyone makes mistakes and that mistakes are growth opportunities. If a leader is a perfectionist, he will not tolerate mistakes from himself or from those that are following. He will likewise fear delegating assignments to others because he thinks he is the only one that can produce perfect results.

15. Ask yourself if this person is your assignment and make adjustments, if necessary.

Just because a person has leadership potential does not mean that you are the person that has been assigned to develop him/her. Ask the Lord for clarity. If you begin working with an emerging leader and notice that this is a "bad fit" be prepared to re-assess and alter the relationship, if necessary.

16. Don't expect the emerging leader not to make mistakes.

What should be expected is an emerging transformational leader that is willing to grow and learn. We are not perfect and are forever learning and growing ourselves.

Just remember that everything reproduces after its own kind. Are you a transformational leader? Have you been accused of transformational thinking? If so, I hope that you are found "GUILTY AS CHARGED!"

BIBLIOGRAPHY

Bass, Bernard & Avolio, Bruce, (1994). Improving organizational effectiveness through transformational leadership. CA: Sage Publication

Bass, Bernard. (1985). Leadership and performance beyond expectations. NY: Free Press

Beardsley, Lisa. (2004). Spiritual Intelligence and the Bible. CA: Loma Linda University

Burns, James MacGregor. (2003). Transforming leadership. NY: Grove Press

Clark, Jonas. (2011). Christian living and spiritual growth; unlocking your prophetic imagination. FL: Spirit of Life Ministries

Csikszentmihalyi, M. (1996). Creativity: Flow and the psychology of discovery and invention. NY: HarperCollins.

Downton, J.V. (1973). Rebel leadership: commitment and charisma in revolutionary process. New York: The Free Press.

Ellison, C. G., Boardman, J. D., Williams, D. R. & Jackson, J. S.(2001). Religious involvement, stress, and mental health: findings from the 1995 Detroit Area Study. Social Forces, 80(1), 215-249.

Foster, Richard. (1998). Streams of living water: essential practices from the six great traditions of Christian faith. New York: Harper Collins Publishers

Fowler, J. W. (1995) Stages of faith: the psychology of human development. San Francisco: Harper.

Gardener, H. (1983). Frames of mind: The theory of multiple intelligences. New York: Basic Books.

Gardner, Howard. (1993). Creating minds: an anatomy of creativity seen through the lives of Freud, Einstein, Picasso, Stravinsky, Eliot, Graham, and Gandhi. NY: Basic Books.

Goleman, D. (1995). Emotional intelligence. New York: Bantam Books.

Greenleaf, Robert K. (1970). The servant as a leader. Essay https://greenleaf.org/products-page/the-servant-as-leader/

Hartley, R.V.L. (1928). Bell Technical Journal. Volume 7, pp. 535-563

Jacobsen, Douglas & Jacobsen, R. H. (2004). Scholarship and Christian faith: enlarging the conversation. NY: Oxford University Press

Journal of School Psychology, Vol.38, No.1, pp. 3-7, 2000. DiLalle, L.F. Theories of Intelligence

Koenig, H. G. (2001). Impact of belief on immune function. Mod. Asp. Immunobiolo. 1(5), 187-190.

Koenig, H. G. (2002). An 83-year-old woman with chronic illness and strong religious beliefs: JAMA, July 24/31, 288(4), 487-493.

Lacayo, R. (May 3, 1993). In the grip of a psychopath. Time Magazine. www.rickross.com/reference/waco/waco12.html

Lee, J., Stacey, G., & Fraser, G. (2003). Social support, religiosity, other psychological factors, and health. In G. E. Fraser, Diet, life expectancy, and chronic disease: studies of Seventh-day Adventists and other vegetarians, pp. 149-176. NY: Oxford University Press.

Mayer, J. D. & Geher, G. (1996). Emotional intelligence and the identification of emotion. Intelligence, 22, 89-113.

Mayer, J. D. & Salovey, P. (1993). The intelligence of emotional intelligence. Intelligence, 17(4), 433-442.

Mayer, J. D. & Salovey, P. (1995). Emotional intelligence and the construction and regulation of feelings. Applied and Preventive Psychology, 4, 197-208.

Molnar, K.(2015).ThinkingErrors.http://www.kmolnar.com/ThinkingErrors.html

Mueller, P. S., Plevak, D. J. & Rummans, T. A. (2001). Religious involvement, spirituality, and medicine: implications for clinical practice. Mayo Clinical Proceedings; 76, 1225-1235.

Musgrave, C. F., Allen, C. E. & Allen, G. J. (2002). Spirituality and health for women of color. American Journal of Public Health, 92(4), 557-560).

Palmer, P. J. (1998). The courage to teach: exploring the inner landscape of a teacher's life. San Francisco: Jossey-Bass.

Payne, W. L. (1985). A study of emotion: developing emotional intelligence; self- integration; relating to fear, pain and desire (theory, structure of reality, problem-solving, contraction/expansion, turning in/coming out/letting go). Doctoral dissertation for the Union for Experimenting Colleges and Universities, Cincinnati, OH.

Phillips. J. B. (1962). Phillips New Testament in Modern English. New York: Harper Collins.

Pinnock, C. H. (1999). Flame of love: a theology of the Holy Spirit. Downers Grove, IL: Intervarsity Press.

Root-Bernstein, R. and Root-Bernstein, M. (1999). Sparks of genius. Boston: Houghton Mifflin.

Salovey, P. & Mayer, J. D.(1990). Emotional intelligence. Imagination, Cognition, and Personality, 9, 185-11.

Schulweis, H. M. (1996). The mismeasurement of man: the quest for spiritual intelligence. http://www.vbs.org/rabbi/hshulw/measure.htm

Spearman, Charles, (1904). General Intelligence. Wikipedia

Spears, Larry C. (2002). Focus on leadership: servant leadership for the twenty first century. NY: John Wiley & Sons

Taylor, B. (2003). Sola Scriptura: lost in translation. Spectrum, 31(4),n 6-9.

Thompson, James W. (2006). Pastoral ministry according to Paul: A biblical vision. Grand Rapids, MI: Baker Academics

Vygotsky, L. S., edited by M. Cole, V. John-Steiner, S. Scribner, & E. Souberman, E. (1978). Mind in society: The development of higher psychological processes. Cambridge, MA: Harvard University Press.

White, E. G. (1952). Education: mountain view. CA: Pacific Press Publishing Association

CPSIA information can be obtained at www.ICGtesting.com
Printed in the USA
BVOW02s1339070715

407620BV00003B/3/P